Bean Cuisine

Janet Horsley

Illustrations by Andrew Pomeroy

AVERY PUBLISHING GROUP INC.
Garden City Park, New York

Published in the United Kingdom in 1982 by
PRISM PRESS, Bridport, Dorset.

Copyright   1982 Janet Horsley

First U.S. Edition, 1989

ISBN 0-89529-446-X

Printed in the United States of America

10 9 8 7

Contents

Introduction

There is no doubt that interest in bean cuisine has been increasing in recent years. Many more shops are stocking dried pulses and there can be few kitchens without jars of beans brightening up the shelves. The reasons for this renewed enthusiasm include economic and ecological considerations, the trend towards natural wholefoods and a growing number of cooks who are prepared to be adventurous.

Many people are aware that beans are highly nutritious, cheap and easy to store but they have difficulty using them in attractive, appetising meals. I hope that this book will help to overcome such problems. It outlines the historical, nutritional and economic aspects of bean cooking and includes an illustrated guide to the common varieties which will enable you to identify them easily and appreciate their individual culinary qualities. The practical details of soaking, cooking and freezing pulses are described and you will be able to learn how to grow your own bean sprouts. Finally there is an extensive recipe section that will be useful to the experienced cook and novice alike. Most of the recipes have been created especially for this book although some are based on traditional dishes from all over the world.

I believe that food should be both appetising and nourishing. Natural, wholesome ingredients are included in all the recipes. Those of you who have yet to use beans have many delights in store, for I am sure that you will be pleasantly surprised by the tastiness and appeal of bean cuisine.

Beans — Past, Present and Future

Historical Context

Beans, peas and lentils belong to the *Leguminosae* family — all members of which bear their seeds in pods. The species that are cultivated for food are collectively referred to as pulses, from the Latin 'puls' meaning pudding or pottage.

Legumes have been grown throughout the world for the past 10,000 years. Some have been in cultivation for so long that they can no longer be found in a wild form. The reasons for this successful record are threefold. Firstly, they yield large quantities of edible seeds which can be either eaten fresh, or dried for use in times of shortage. Secondly, there are over 14,000 species in the family and although only twenty two are grown in any quantity for human consumption they thrive in a wide range of climatic conditions. The soya bean needs warmth, pigeon peas prefer the hot, humid tropics, the haricot bean thrives in Mediterranean climates and the butter bean, by far the hardiest, can tolerate colder, temperate latitudes. Finally, legumes play an important role in the farming practice known as crop rotation. This is because they have the ability to absorb nitrogen from the air into their root systems. This not only results in high yields from relatively poor land but it also leaves the soil more fertile than before.

It is easy to see why legumes have been cultivated since the earliest of times, but they have not always been a popular food. Many myths and folklores have grown up around them. The following are a few examples.

Egyptian priests in the period around 500 B.C. regarded broad beans as unclean, believing them to contain the souls of dead men. The great Greek mathematician, Pythagoras, also refused to eat them because they were said to cause insomnia and nightmares. Perhaps his obvious dislike of beans gave rise to the legend surrounding his death. It is said that while escaping from Dionysus he suddenly came upon a field of beans, and rather than risk crossing such an obstacle, he surrendered to his pursuers.

Apollo, the Greek sun god, is said to have been responsible for making the fruits of the earth ripen, protecting the crops by destroying mice and driving off locusts. The Greeks duly paid their respects to his services and sacrificed the first of the year's crops in his honour. They also celebrated his name by holding 'bean feasts'!

The Bible contains many references to pulses and lentils. In the Old Testament, Esau came to his brother from the fields and asked for food, to which Jacob replied, 'sell me this day thy birthright'. So near to starvation was Esau that he agreed to pay this high price and duly received some bread and a pottage of red lentils.

The story of Daniel at the court of the King of Babylon gives a glowing account of the nutritional value of beans. It says that the King, Nebuchadnezzar, decided to look after the 'royal' children of Israel and feed them on the King's meat and wine to ensure that they grew up strong and healthy. One of these children, Daniel, insisted on eating only pulse and water. His guardian, fearing the wrath of the King should illness befall the child, reluctantly agreed to a trial period of ten days. At the end of this period Daniel's 'countenance appeared fairer and fatter in flesh' than those children fed on the meat and wine.

With the introduction of such foods as the potato and maize from the New World in the sixteenth century the humble bean once again fell out of favour. It came to be regarded as a poor man's food to be eaten out of necessity rather than choice. Fortunately for the bean's flagging popularity, travellers from Central and South America brought back the French and Runner beans. At first, these plants were grown for their delicate flowers and attractive foliage but soon their delicious seed pods were being served at the tables of Charles II of England and Louis XIV of France.

Thus the popularity of pulses has fluctuated throughout the course of history. At the present time they are experiencing something of a revival and many different types of fresh, dried and canned beans are available. This is a welcome development for the bean remains an economic and highly nutritious food.

Nutritional Background

During recent years beans have been underrated and in the Western world they are rarely taken seriously as an important supplier of nutrients. Yet they have a higher protein content than milk, eggs, meat or fish and are an important source of dietary fibre.

Food consists of five principal nutrients — *protein, carbohydrates, fat, vitamins* and *minerals*. Although they are all equally important protein has come to be regarded as the most valuable of them all. Its prime function is to build and repair body tissues. The popular idea that protein is the most important nutrient may have arisen from our need to eat it regularly because of the body's inability to store surplus amounts. There is however no benefit in eating it to excess. Food scientists agree that in the West we eat two to three times more protein than our bodies can utilise.

There is a basic difference between first class (animal) and second class (vegetable) proteins. Nowadays these are referred to as 'complete' and 'incomplete' proteins respectively. All proteins are made up of twenty two amino acids, fourteen

	Carbo-hydrates	Proteins	Fat	Fibre	Vitamins + Minerals	Water
Kidney bean	55	24	2	5	2	12
Milk	4	4	4	0	1	87
Eggs	1	12	12	0	1	74
Beef steak	0	18	17	0	1	64
White fish	0	17.25	0.25	0	1.25	81.25
Brown rice	76	7	2	2	2	11
Whole wheat	71	13	2	2	2	10

Table showing percentage comparison of nutrients

of which can be manufactured within the body. The remaining eight are known as essential amino acids and must be obtained from our diet. Foods that do not contain the correct balance or are lacking in one or more of the essential amino acids are known as 'incomplete' proteins. They tend to be vegetable in origin and include most beans, grains, nuts and seeds. The soya bean, however, yields a 'complete' protein and is on a par with other 'complete' protein foods such as meat, fish, eggs and dairy products.

The imbalance in the 'incomplete' vegetable proteins can be corrected simply by eating two kinds of these foods at the same meal, it is not necessary to count the animo acid content of every food. In the kitchen it is sufficient to serve two or more 'incomplete' protein foods at each meal. For example, the amino acids in whole grains complement those in pulses giving a combined protein equal in quality to that of any 'complete' protein food. Remember too that many meals include dairy foods which, in themselves, provide a complete range of amino acids.

Complementing vegetable proteins is easy and natural. It is in fact the basis of many traditional cuisines — the combination of dhal and chapatties in India, kidney beans and tortillas in Mexico, hummus and pitta bread in the Middle East and bean sprouts and noodles in China are all excellent examples.

In the West there is no need for concern regarding either the quality or quantity of protein. Provided that a variety of foods are eaten and the intake of calories matches your requirements the body's own regulatory mechanisms can take care of the rest.

The good levels of protein and dietary fibre

and the low fat content of beans makes them excellent food for inclusion in anyone's diet. The fact that they are also rich in the B vitamins, thiamine and niacin, and in calcium and iron is just an added bonus!

international cuisine shows that they can be used in many attractive and delicious dishes. Recent interest in wholefood cookery has resulted in a further increase in the range of recipes available for the adventurous cook.

Economic Considerations

The developed countries have only a quarter of the world's population yet in 1970 they consumed three quarters of all its grain supplies and fish catch. Much of this food was fed to animals; ten pounds of vegetable protein being required to produce one pound of animal protein.

The crop failures in 1973 made it obvious that world agriculture could not be relied upon to produce sufficient food to feed livestock and the human population. Consequently agronomists have been investigating the possibility of growing more pulses for direct human consumption. This would have advantages because beans are simple to grow, do not need prime land or large applications of artificial fertilizers and can be produced in a wide range of climatic conditions. They are also easy to handle and store and involve very little wastage.

The attempt to revolutionise our eating habits by producing simulated meat products from soya beans has apparently failed through consumer resistance. There seems however to be a renewed interest in using the whole beans themselves in cooking. The use of pulses in

The A–Z of Beans

One of the difficulties experienced by the bean cook is to identify the different beans available. This section describes the more common types, including the colloquial names, distinguishing features, special nutritional qualities, culinary uses, complementary foods and seasonings.

An appreciation of the variety of beans available and of their individual flavours and qualities opens up whole new areas of cooking. With the help of the information in this book you will be able to leave those days of 'beans on toast' far behind.

Aduki Bean (*Phaseolus angularis*)

The aduki bean is small, round and reddish brown in colour. It is grown throughout the Far East, being popular in China and Japan where it is known as the 'King of the Beans'. It is sometimes referred to as the feijao, adzuki or azuki bean.

Adukis have a light, nutty flavour that enhances both savoury and sweet dishes. In Japan they are made into candied bean cakes which are served with green leaf tea at the end of a meal. They are also cooked with rice in a dish called aduki meshi or red rice because it takes on the delicate pink colouring of the beans.

Reputed to be a gift from a benevolent god to an evil world, the aduki is said to have beneficial effects upon the kidneys. More importantly however, it is an excellent source of protein, the B group vitamins and iron.

Black Bean (*Phaseolus vulgaris*)

A shiny, black, kidney-shaped bean which is used extensively in South American and Caribbean cooking. A black bean soup traditionally made in Cuba and Puerto Rico is seasoned with cumin, garlic, oregano and lemon juice. The black bean has a subtle mushroom flavour and is particularly good in soups and casseroles. It is also known by the names 'turtle soup bean', 'Mexican Blacks' and 'frijoles negros'

Blackeye Bean (*Vigna unguiculata*)

As their name suggests blackeye beans are small, creamy-white in colour and have a black mark at the sprouting point. This easily recognizable marking has resulted in them being nicknamed 'blackeyed suzies'. They are also known as the cow pea and blackeye pea.

Blackeye beans have a pleasant savoury flavour and a light texture, and become pinkish when cooked. They have a thinner skin than many other beans and cook quickly without need for soaking. It is thought that these beans originated in Africa but they can now be found growing throughout the tropics, especially in the southern states of America. The young pods can be eaten as a fresh vegetable and the plant's leafy shoots are reputed to taste like spinach. The dried beans are best when cooked and served with rice, local vegetables and fresh herbs.

Broad Bean (*Vicia faba*)

When fresh, broad beans are easily recognizable in their green pods but in the dried form they are a large, flattish bean, creamy-brown in colour. The wrinkled skin is tough even after cooking and they are best used as a purée in soups, pâtés and pies.

The broad bean is thought to have been the first legume to be cultivated in the Old World, and traces have been found in Bronze Age sites in Switzerland and among Iron Age remains in Britain. A favourite snack for the children of Eastern Europe was said to be a handful of broad beans, still warm from the cooking pot. In more recent years they have been found to

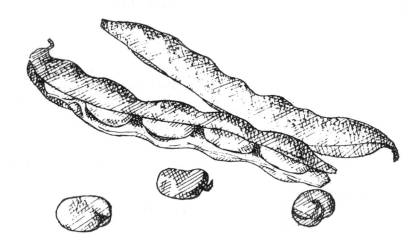

cause a blood disorder, known as favism, in people with a specific allergy. However this condition is rare and is found principally among the Mediterranean people.

Broad beans are called wax beans or fava beans in some parts of the world.

Butter Bean (*Phaseolus lunatus*)

There are two main species of butter bean: a large variety known as the lima bean coming from Peru; and a smaller one, from Mexico, known as the sieva bean. Both are classed under the the family name *Phaseolus lunatus* and may be referred to as the Madagascar, curry or pole bean. There is no difference between the two as far as their taste, texture and creamy-white colour are concerned but the baby butter bean or sieva bean cooks much quicker.

Originating in South America the butter bean became a staple food of the American Indians. Its smooth texture and savoury flavour are complemented perfectly by fresh sweetcorn in the traditional dish known as Succotash.

Canellini Bean (*Phaseolus vulgaris*)

A member of the haricot bean family, the canellini bean was first cultivated in Argentina. It is now commercially grown in Italy and is sometimes referred to as the fazolia bean.

The canellini is white, oval in shape, smooth in texture and has a slightly nutty flavour. It is larger than the haricot bean but can be used in similar recipes.

Chick Pea (*Cicer arietinum*)

Widely grown in India, Burma and the Middle East the chick pea is also called garbanzo and bengal gram. It is highly nutritious, being rich in protein, fat, calcium, iron and the B group of vitamins. The chick pea vaguely resembles the garden pea in shape and size, but it is buff coloured and has a crinkly skin. Well liked by both meat eaters and vegetarians, its rich, full flavour can enhance any pâté, pie, casserole or curry.

Native to the Mediterranean area the chick pea is used widely in traditional Greek and North African cuisines and is the principal ingredient in the popular spread known as hummus. This dish is made from the puréed chick peas, tahini, oil and lemon juice. It is eaten as a starter or a snack with pitta bread and black olives.

Field Bean (*Vicia faba*)

Belonging to the broad bean family this is one of the few beans to be grown successfully in colder, temperate climates. The field bean is mid-brown, small and round, with a tough skin which is rather indigestible. For this reason it has never been particularly popular and is best used as a purée in soups and pies.

Colloquial names include the British horse bean, tic and daffa bean.

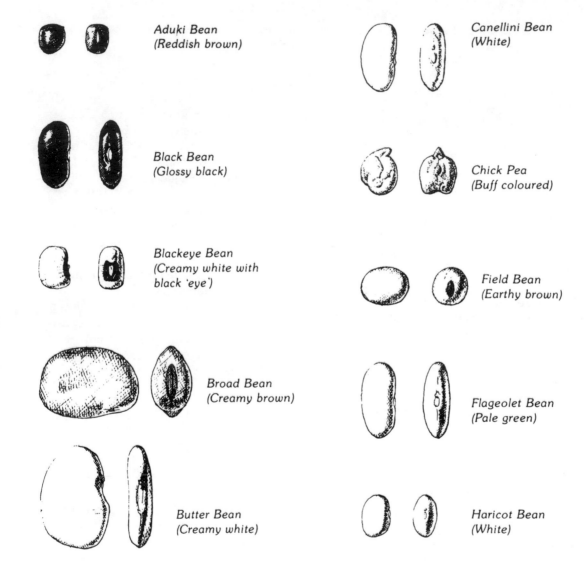

Aduki Bean
(Reddish brown)

Canellini Bean
(White)

Black Bean
(Glossy black)

Chick Pea
(Buff coloured)

Blackeye Bean
(Creamy white with
black 'eye')

Field Bean
(Earthy brown)

Broad Bean
(Creamy brown)

Flageolet Bean
(Pale green)

Butter Bean
(Creamy white)

Haricot Bean
(White)

An illustrated guide to beans

Kidney Bean
(Glossy red)

  Mung Bean
(Olive green)

 Split Pea
(Yellow)

  Red Lentil
(Orange)

    Pinto Bean
(Pinkish–buff flecked with beige and pink)

  Brown Lentil
(Pale reddish brown)

  Rosecoco Bean
(Deep pink. flecked with beige and brown)

  Green Lentil
(Pale green/brown with orange/brown edges)

  Soya Bean
Light creamy–yellow)

Marrowfat Pea
(Pale green)

Flageolet Bean (*Phaseolus vulgaris*)

Flageolet beans are regarded as something of a delicacy in the bean world. Removed from the pod as immature seeds they are very tender and have a light refreshing taste. They are smaller than a kidney bean but similarly shaped and are often included in recipes because of their attractive, pale green colouring.

Cultivated mainly in France and Italy, flageolets are traditionally eaten cold, tossed in a herby vinaigrette dressing and accompanying other salad dishes.

Haricot Bean (*Phaseolus vulgaris*)

Haricots are probably the best known of all the beans, popularized by H.J. Heinz of Pittsburgh. In their natural state haricots are small, white, oval shaped beans, sometimes referred to as the Great Northern bean and the American Navy bean. They can be found in traditional dishes from the Middle East, Italy, France and Greece. The Americans have made them popular in a variety of ways. As well as the familiar bean cooked in tomato sauce, an old fashioned dish, called Boston Baked Beans, uses mustard and molasses as its main seasonings.

Kidney Bean (*Phaseolus vulgaris*)

The best known variety of kidney bean is the glossy red Wonder, Chilli or Mexican bean. It is possible to buy brown, black and white varieties but they are not so commonly available. All kidney beans are good sources of protein and iron.

Rich in flavour and colour the red kidney bean is popular throughout the world and can be found in all types of cuisine. Most famous perhaps is its use in the South American dish, chilli con carne. It is a native bean of the West Indies, where it is traditionally cooked with rice, coconut milk, onions, hot peppers and fresh thyme.

Lentil (*Lens esculenta*)

One of the first legumes to be eaten by man, reference is made to the lentil in the Old Testament. It is thought that Roman Catholics used to eat them during Lent and this may have had some bearing upon their name. However, it is more likely to derive from the Latin word 'Lens', a reference to the shape of the bean.

There are many varieties of this plant grown throughout the world. The green, brown and red lentils are the most common types available in the West. The red split lentil is best cooked to a smooth purée and used as a base for stews, soups and pies. The green or brown lentil can be either puréed or cooked just to the point of tenderness and used whole. The green lentil (or Egyptian lentil, as it is also referred to) has a light, fresh flavour which is enhanced by herb seasonings and is excellent served cold with salads. The brown lentil, or the smaller Chinese lentil, has an 'earthier' taste and makes a good extender, or substitute for meat, in such dishes as spaghetti bolognese and shepherd's pie.

It is said that the lentil's high protein content is more easily digested than that of the larger beans. They play a vital role in the diet of many under-developed nations and feature strongly in the recipes of Asian and North African countries.

Mung Bean (*Phaseolus aureus*)

The mung bean is thought to have originated in India where it is also known as the green gram. It is a small, round, olive green bean that can be used whole or it can be sprouted. The tender young pods are eaten too, as a fresh green vegetable.

The mung bean is especially rich in vitamins A and B and has five times as much food value after it has been sprouted. The beansprout is also much easier to digest and assimilate than the actual bean for during the germination the starches are broken down into simple sugars, the proteins into amino acids and the fats into fatty acids. The 'miracle' does not stop there, new vitamins are actually formed. Beansprouts are the only source of vitamin C and vitamin B_{12} to be found in pulses.

The black gram or urd is a member of the same family and is indigenous to Africa, Asia and the West Indies. Mung beans should not be mistaken for pigeon peas or red grams which are red beans of similar shape and size. The pigeon pea is a member of the *Cajanus* family but can be used in similar recipes to the mung bean.

Peas (*Pisum sativum*)

Peas are said to have originated in the Garden of Eden. They are known to have been grown by the Romans and were used throughout the Middle Ages in Europe, generally being dried and stored for use in the winter in such dishes as the Old English 'Pease Pudding'.

Fresh garden peas were not eaten until the seventeenth century. They were received with great enthusiasm in France at the time of Louis XIV. A letter written by Madame de Maintenon on May 16th 1696 records their popularity:

'the anticipation of eating them,
the pleasure of eating them and
the delight of eating them again
were the three main topics discussed
by our princes for the last four days'.

Nor does the popularity of the garden pea seem to have declined. It is now possible to eat green peas every day of the year thanks to modern food technology. The dried marrowfat is considered very much its poor relation, but it is important to remember that its flavour and texture are very different from those of the fresh pea and that it is still a very useful food in its own right.

Split peas are more frequently used in cooking nowadays for they need no soaking and cook quickly. They make an excellent basis for nourishing, warming winter soups and stews. Green split peas are best seasoned with herbs and the 'musty', savoury taste of the yellow variety can be livened up with eastern spices.

Pinto Bean (*Phaseolus vulgaris*)

Pinto beans are kidney shaped and have a pale, whitish skin mottled with shades of beige and pink. When cooked they become a uniform pink colour and look most attractive and succulent. Pinto beans are traditionally grown in Latin America and are delicious eaten cold with a selection of salads.

Rosecoco Bean (*Phaseolus vulgaris*)

Rosecoco beans are very similar in shape, taste, texture and appearance to the pinto bean and the two types can be substituted, one for another, in most recipes. Rosecocoes are kidney shaped with a deep pink skin, flecked with beige and brown and are also called borlotti, salugia and crab eye beans.

They come from South America where it is the common practice to cook a large pot full of beans and to reheat them in smaller amounts when needed. For this reason the Mexicans call them frijoles refritas and re-awakening beans.

Soya Bean (*Glycine max*)

The soya or soy bean has been a staple food in the Far East for over 5,000 years and it is even referred to as 'the meat of the soil'. It is the most nutritious of all the beans, having a protein content equal in quality to that of animal protein foods. It is also a good source of fat, lecithin, vitamins A, B and E, calcium, potassium and phosphorus.

Round in shape and about the size of a pea the soya bean is usually light creamy-yellow although it is possible to find black, green and brown varieties. It is reputed to be the hardest bean and it is hardly surprising that it needs a lengthy soak prior to being cooked.

As there is no tradition in Oriental cuisine for slow, casserole-type dishes which would provide ample time for the bean to soften, the Chinese and Japanese, with their quicker cooking methods, have devised many ways of preparing the soya bean in order that its complete protein can be utilized to the full.

Soya sauce, a dark rich liquid, is a principal seasoning used in Oriental cooking. It is reputed to strengthen and stimulate the digestive juices. Naturally-fermented or 'brewed' soya sauce is made from soya beans, wheat and sea salt and is superior in flavour and nutrients to many of the 'commercial' brands available in the West. There is an easy test for checking the authenticity of soya sauce. Simply shake the bottle until bubbles form on the top. A naturally-fermented sauce will produce lots of 'fizz' that may take up to a minute to disperse. Soya sauce can go under the name 'shoyu' or 'tamari' both of which are of the best quality. 'Tamari' is a slightly thicker, richer liquid than 'shoyu' and is used in smaller amounts.

Soya sauce is an excellent addition to most savoury dishes and can be used in soups, stir-fries, rice dishes, casseroles, pies and salads. The real problem is not when to use it but when to leave it out of recipes.

Soya paste or *miso* is another fermented product originating in Japan. It has a mellow, fruity flavour and can be used in sweet and savoury dishes. It is a highly concentrated food containing 'complete' proteins, vitamin B and bacteria that are beneficial to the digestive system. It is an excellent food for convalescents. In Japan it is customary to start the day with a bowl of miso soup and here the saying goes, 'miso *every day keeps the doctor away*'!

To retain all the miso's nutritional qualities it must not be boiled, and is best added to dishes just before serving. It will keep indefinitely in a cool place, its flavour sometimes ripening and improving with age.

Bean curd or *tofu* is sold in Chinese delicatessens and some wholefood shops. It is a white, curd-like solid also called soya cheese. Rich in protein, vitamins and minerals whilst being low in saturated fat, carbohydrates and calories, it is a really outstanding food.

Tofu is rather bland in flavour and is best combined with other foods. Try making your own and season it with herbs, garlic or spring onions.

Recipe for home-made tofu:

Blend 8 oz soya flour and 1½ pints of cold water together. Add a pint of boiling water and bring to the boil. Simmer gently for 1 hour before stirring in the juice of two lemons. Leave the mixture to cool. Strain through a cloth and pack into a container when it has become solid.

Soya flour is a yellow flour, high in protein and low in gluten. It can enrich and lighten breads, pastries and stocks and can be used as an egg substitute in cakes and batters: one dessertspoon of flour being the equivalent of one egg. The flour is strong-flavoured and should be used in small amounts. 2-3 ozs of soya flour to 1 lb of wheat flour is an ideal proportion.

Soya milk is another product devised by the ingenious Chinese. It is richer in iron, calcium and phosphorous than cow's milk and can be used in baking, desserts and beverages. In some parts of China soya milk is delivered to the door by a milkman! Commercial brands of soya milk are available in many shops and it is possible to make it at home.

Recipe for home-made soya milk:

Soak 8 oz of soya beans for 12 hours. Drain and grind them to a pulp. Mix in 2 pints of cold water and bring to the boil. Simmer gently for 2 hours and then strain off the milk. Store in a cool place.

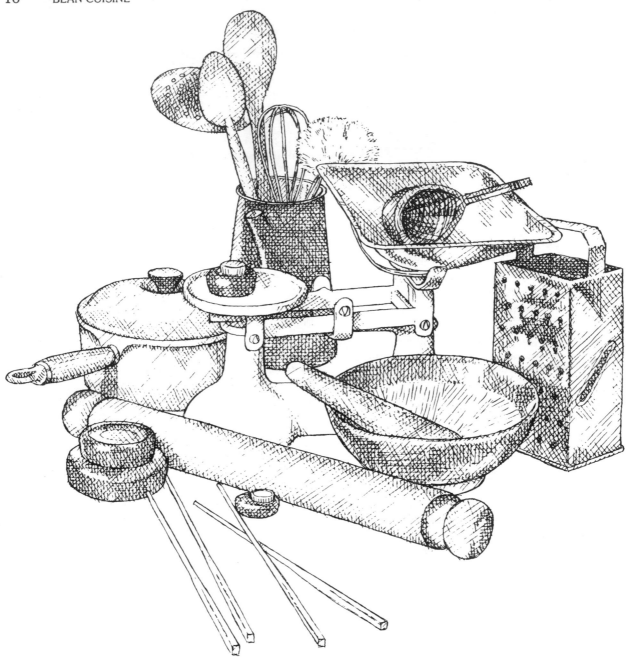

Basic Cookery Guide

The recipes in this book have been chosen to suit every occasion. The recipe section contains many wholesome dishes that are economical and simple to prepare, and a selection of more unusual ideas that will appeal to the adventurous cook. No special equipment or knowledge of cooking is needed to prepare these mouth-watering meals.

The main difficulty experienced by the novice bean cook is that of meal planning, as most people have been brought up to think in terms of meat and two vegetables. An attempt to plan a meal around a plate of boiled beans might tax the imagination of even the greatest cook! Beans are seldom cooked and served on their own; vegetables and seasonings play a very important role and can turn a simple dish of beans into a meal fit for a king. To help you adapt to this style of cooking, serving suggestions accompany each recipe and should enable you to provide attractive, nutritious and appetising meals.

Bean cooking has the reputation of being a lengthy, time consuming operation. The busy cook, who finds it difficult to plan meals in advance, will be glad to learn that black eye beans, lentils and split peas need no soaking and can be cooked in a very short time. Tins of cooked beans can be bought in many shops but seldom have the flavour and colour of pulses prepared in the home. They tend to be very soft, and disintegrate if added to slow-cooking casseroles and stews. In addition, they generally contain synthetic additives, preservatives, salt and sugar. Whilst they are useful in an emergency it is best to adopt the habit of keeping a wide selection of dried pulses in the larder for everyday use.

Beans are highly nutritious and to maximize their food value the recipes combine them with other natural ingredients. Brown rice, wholewheat flour and wholewheat pasta have textures and flavours which complement those of pulses and, at the same time, they provide additional nutrients and extra dietary roughage. Good quality, unrefined oils should also be used. Soya, sunflower and safflower oils are ideal, having good colour and flavour whilst being relatively inexpensive. The nutty aroma of sesame oil gives an authentic taste to Oriental dishes and olive oil is perfect for all types of Middle East and Mediterranean cuisines.

The amount of seasoning, herbs and spices

added to food is very much a question of personal taste and should be adjusted accordingly. Some of the recipes in this book use soya sauce and miso as seasoning agents. As these two products are naturally salty it is not necessary to add further salt to the food during its preparation.

A brief description of any less well-known ingredients and cooking terms used in the recipes can be found at the end of this chapter.

Equipment

Beans have played an important role in many types of traditional cuisine. Before the advent of cans, freezers and other methods of food preservation, dried beans were an important winter food reserve. The old fashioned kitchen range and hob was an ideal way to cook beans as the pot could be left unattended, to simmer slowly and gently, until its contents were tender and the stock full of flavour.

Although the modern, streamlined kitchen rarely contains such unsophisticated equipment there are now other, equally effective, means of preparing dried pulses.

The basic cooking method is to boil the beans in a pan of water until they become soft and tender. Provided that sufficient water is used, the beans can be left to simmer throughout the recommended cooking period.

The 'slow crock' electric cooking pot seems, at first sight, to be the answer to a busy cook's prayer – a self-contained unit that needs no supervision and can be left all day to cook the

evening meal. However, recent research has shown that this may not be a satisfactory way of preparing pulses. Some beans, notably the red kidney bean, contain toxins which are only destroyed by brisk boiling and they have been known to cause sickness when eaten raw or insufficiently cooked. The temperatures reached in slow cookers may be too low to destroy these natural toxins and it is suggested that pulses should be boiled for 10 minutes before being placed in the slow cooker. It is best to follow the crock-pot manufacturer's instructions when choosing the temperature setting.

By far the most effective method of cooking pulses is in a pressure cooker. Modern designs incorporate very sophisticated safety mechanisms and, provided the pressure cooker is used correctly, there is no risk of an 'explosion'. The initial cost of this piece of equipment may seem rather high but it is an excellent investment and pressure cookers should last for years. They are particularly useful to the bean cook because they save fuel, preserve nutrients and reduce the soaking and cooking times by three-quarters, enabling meals to be prepared quickly and easily.

Some of the recipes state that the beans should be mashed or puréed. This can be done quite easily with a potato masher or a kitchen sieve. Naturally a food blender/grinder does the job more efficiently but it is not essential.

There is a wide range of equipment available for sprouting beans and seeds in the home. Purpose-made containers may need less attention, but they are not really necessary. All that is required is warmth, moisture, air and a container that drains well. Try using a sieve, a clay plant pot lined with blotting paper, or a jam jar. Tie muslin over the opening to stop the beans falling out when rinsing and to help keep them moist. Bean sprouts can be grown in a light or dark place. Extra light increases the vitamin C content but reduces the level of vitamin B_{12}.

How to grow bean sprouts

1. Pick over the beans and discard any broken or discoloured ones which may go mouldy. Approximately 2-3 tablespoons of beans will yield 6-8oz (1½-2 cups) of sprouts.
2. Soak the beans overnight in plenty of luke-warm water.
3. Drain well and place the beans in a clean pot or jar. Stand in a warm place. The optimum temperature for germination is 80°F/27°C but it does not really matter if it falls a little below this. Cooler conditions simply slow down the rate of growth.
4. The sprouts must be rinsed in fresh luke-warm water every morning and evening to keep them moist. Excess water should be drained off thoroughly to ensure that the beans do not rot.
5. After 4-5 days the beansprouts should be ready to eat. Rinse them well to remove any loose skins, which may be leathery, and drain well. They can be stored in a refrigerator for several days but are best used quickly. The nutritional content of the bean sprouts is at its best after 4 days and quickly deteriorates thereafter.

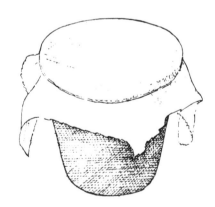

Types of bean sprouts

Type	*Average length after 5 days*	*Comments*
mung beans	1½-2 inches	Widely used in Chinese cooking. Crisp and crunchy.
aduki beans	1-1½ inches	Sweet, succulent and delicately flavoured.
green lentils	½-1 inch	Excellent in salads, a fresh and light texture.
chick peas	1-1½ inches	A large, crisp bean sprout full of flavour.
soya beans	1-1½ inches	The hardness of the bean makes it difficult to sprout. It is best to soak it initially for 24 hours.

Quantities

Most pulses double in size and weight when soaked and cooked while the soya bean and the chick pea increase up to three times. A useful guide is that 8oz (1 cup) of dried beans gives 1-1¼lbs (2-2½ cups) of cooked beans. As there is no fat, bone or gristle to remove an 8oz (1 cup) dry weight is sufficient for four people.

Sorting and Washing

Generally speaking, prepacked beans bought in supermarkets only need to be rinsed lightly before soaking and cooking. Cheaper, loose beans sold directly from the sack may not have been sorted and can contain grit, stones, twigs and seed pods. Red lentils and chick peas are particularly notorious for harbouring small stones, usually the same size as the bean itself. It is a tedious but important task to remove the rubble from your beans, particularly if you do not want to lose both teeth and friends at your next dinner party!

Soaking and Rinsing

Most beans benefit from being soaked, the exceptions are lentils, split peas and blackeye beans. The flatulence problem associated with eating beans is caused by sugars called oligosaccharides. These need to be broken down into a digestible form by thorough cooking before they can be assimilated properly by the body. Soaking the harder, larger beans helps to break down these sugars and also softens the bean thus reducing the overall cooking time.

There are two ways of soaking pulses:

1. The 'short soak' is quick and very useful if you need to cook a meal in a hurry. Wash the beans and place them in a pan of cold water. Bring to the boil and simmer for 15 minutes. Remove from the heat and leave covered for 1-1½ hours. Proceed to cook as instructed.

2. The 'long soak' is much the best method of preparing beans as it improves their digestibility. Cover the beans with at least twice their volume of water and leave to soak for 6–24 hours. The chart on page 23 gives the recommended times for each individual bean. The soaking period can be greatly reduced if the final cooking is done in a pressure cooker.

Very few nutrients are lost during soaking. Some of the oligosaccharides that can cause flatulence may dissolve in the water and it is recommended that after soaking the beans are rinsed and then cooked in fresh water.

Seasoning and Softening Agents

Very old or dry beans may take longer than the recommended cooking times before they become tender. In such circumstances some cooks suggest using baking powder to soften the offending beans. However, the inclusion of baking powder in bean recipes, for whatever purpose, is not recommended as it destroys the B vitamins and can adversely affect the flavour.

Nor should salt or salty seasoning agents be added until the pulses are thoroughly cooked. This is because the 'osmotic' effect of brine retards the absorption of the water by the beans, with the result that the cooking period is lengthened.

Cooking

The simplest method of cooking pulses, having first soaked them for the appropriate length of time, is to place them in a pan with fresh cold water. Bring to the boil, reduce the heat and simmer until the beans are soft and tender. The chart on page 23 gives the recommended cooking times.

If using a pressure cooker it is important to make sure that the pan is no more than half full of ingredients, including liquid. Some pulses, notably soya beans, have a tendency to 'bubble up' through the safety valve while under pressure. This difficulty can be overcome by the addition of one tablespoon of vegetable oil to the ingredients. The oil also stops any loose bean skins from rising and clogging the steam escape valve.

There are two methods of reducing pressure at the end of the cooking period:

1. The 'quick method' — run cold water over the top of the pressure cooker.
2. The 'slow method' — the pan is removed from the heat and left to reduce pressure gradually. The beans continue cooking during this time and it is important to reduce the times shown in the chart by 2-3 minutes.

The beans in common usage are perfectly safe to eat and are an invaluable source of nutrients, but in the modern world of 'fast foods' it is important to realise that, like animal proteins such as meat, fish and eggs, beans need to be cooked thoroughly and that merely softening a bean by soaking is not sufficient.

Bean Stock

The liquid remaining after cooking beans can be used as a stock for casseroles, soups and stews. It is nutritious and full of flavour and should cause little or no flatulence. For those with very poor digestion however, it is probably wise to make fresh stock from cooked vegetables or bouillon cubes.

Storing and Freezing

The dried bean is a naturally-preserved food and is best stored in its natural state. However it is sometimes useful to prepare more beans than

are actually needed for a particular meal and to keep them for an occasion when time may be at a premium. Soaked or cooked beans can be stored for several days in a refrigerator. Cooked bean dishes may also be kept for a short time in a cool place such as a larder or refrigerator, and for much longer in a freezer. Beans freeze very well and it is always useful to have a supply of bean burgers, nut rolls, red kidney bean quiches and date loaves in the freezer to fall back on in times of great need or laziness!

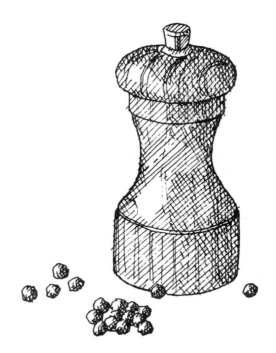

Cooking Times

The recommended times can only be approximate and should be used as a rough guide.

	Simmering		Pressure Cooking (15lbs)	
Type of bean	Soaking Time	Cooking Time	Soaking Time	Cooking Time
Aduki beans	overnight	¾-1 hour	6 hours	10 minutes
Black beans	overnight	1-1½ hours	6 hours	10 minutes
Blackeye beans	-	¾-1 hour	-	8 minutes
Broad beans	overnight	1½-2 hours	6 hours	15 minutes
Butter beans	overnight	1½-2 hours	6 hours	15 minutes
Canellini beans	overnight	1-1½ hours	6 hours	10 minutes
Chick peas	overnight	2-2½ hours	6 hours	25 minutes
Field beans	overnight	1-1½ hours	6 hours	10 minutes
Flageolet beans	overnight	1-1½ hours	6 hours	10 minutes
Haricot beans	overnight	1-1½ hours	6 hours	10 minutes
Kidney beans	overnight	1-1½ hours	6 hours	15 minutes
Lentils — brown	-	¾-1 hour	-	8 minutes
Lentils — green	-	¾-1 hour	-	8 minutes
Lentils — red	-	¾ hour	-	6–8 minutes
Mung beans	overnight	¾-1 hour	6 hours	10 minutes
Peas — marrowfat	overnight	1-1½ hours	6 hours	10 minutes
Peas — split	-	¾-1 hour	-	8 minutes
Pinto beans	overnight	1-1½ hours	6 hours	10 minutes
Rosecoco beans	overnight	1-1½ hours	6 hours	10 minutes
Soya beans	24 hours	3-3½ hours	24 hours	25 minutes

Cooking Terms and Ingredients

Arrowroot	A fine, white powder from the arrowroot plant, which is used as a thickening agent. When heated with water it gives a firm, clear jelly that is good for puddings and fruit flans.
Blind baking	A term used to describe the baking of a pastry case without a filling.
Brown rice	Also known as unpolished rice. It has a stronger flavour, is superior in food value and is easier to digest than white or 'pearled' varieties. It also contains valuable dietary fibre which is absent from white rice. Both long and short grain rice can be used in savoury dishes. Use whichever type you prefer.
Buckwheat spaghetti	A whole grain spaghetti made from buckwheat. It is also known as soba.
Croûtons	Small squares of fried bread used as a garnish.
Dry roasting	Roasting food in an oven without any fat. The food can be cooked in a similar fashion in a pan on the stove-top or under the grill. It is used mainly in the preparation of nuts, seeds and whole grains.
Garam masala	A blend of coriander, black pepper, caraway, cloves, cardamom and cinnamon.
Gelatine	A clear setting agent used to make jellies and fruit desserts. Gelatine is made from animal products and vegetarians may wish to use arrowroot, agar-agar or carrageen instead.
Ghee	Clarified butter used widely in Indian cooking.
Herbs	The quantities given in the recipes are for dried herbs. Fresh varieties have a much 'truer', and more pleasant, flavour but need to be used in larger amounts. Approximately 1 tablespoon of fresh herbs is equivalent to 1 teaspoon of dried herbs.
Honey	Honey is used as the sweetening agent in some of the recipes. The use of brown and white sugar should be avoided as both are highly refined with little nutritional value.
Julienne strips	Delicately cut vegetables in the shape of matchsticks.
Mace	The husk surrounding the nutmeg. Available in blade and powdered form.
Maize meal	A fine, yellow flour milled from maize. It is also called corn meal.
Oat flakes	Jumbo oats.

Oil	The best oils are cold pressed as they retain their natural flavour and essential nutrients. They may also be sold as 'unrefined' or 'virgin' oil.
Par boiling	Boiling for a short time to partially cook the food.
Porridge oats	Rolled or quick cooking oats.
Sake	A Japanese rice wine which is a principal ingredient in Oriental cooking. Dry sherry may be used in its place.
Salt	Although some salt is essential to good health most people eat far too much. It is said to be a contributory factor in heart disease and hypertension. Season foods lightly and use naturally salted soya sauce and miso in place of refined table or sea salt.
Stir-fry	A method of frying food quickly using a minimum amount of oil.
Tahini	A spread made from sesame seeds. It is also known as 'creamed sesame', 'sesame cream' and 'sesame butter'.
Tomato purée	Tomato paste.
Unbleached white flour	100% wholewheat flour should normally be used in the kitchen. Occasionally, however, it is useful to have a lighter, refined flour for making some types of sauces and pastries. Choose an 'unbleached' variety that contains no additives or bleaching agents. Don't be surprised if it looks dirty in comparison to its 'whiter than white' counterparts.
Unleavened bread	Bread made without any raising agents.
Wholewheat flour	This is the best flour to use in terms of flavour, nutritional value and dietary roughage. As the name suggests it contains every part of the whole wheat grain. It is available coarsely ground for making bread, finer ground for pastries, and as a self-raising flour for cakes and puddings.

British/American Food Terms

British	American
Aubergine	Eggplant
Baking tin	Cake pan
Baking tray	Cookie sheet
Bean/pulse	Bean/legume
Biscuits	Cookies/crackers
Cake tin	Cake pan
Chinese leaves	Chinese cabbage
Courgette	Zucchini
Desiccated coconut	Dried coconut
Frying pan	Skillet
French bean	Green/string bean
Marrowfat pea	Soup pea
Porridge oats	Rolled oats/quick-cooking oats
Scone	Biscuit
Soya bean	Soy bean
Spring onions	Scallions
To grill	To broil
To mince	To grind
Watercress	Similar to landcress
Yeast Extract	Savita

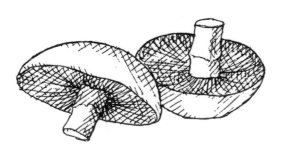

British/American Conversion Tables

British	American
1 teaspoon (tsp) —level	1 teaspoon — heaped
1 dessertspoon (dessertsp) — level	1 dessertspoon — heaped
1 tablespoon (tbsp) — level	1 tablespoon — heaped
8 fluid ounces (fl oz)	1 U.S. cup
16 fluid ounces (fl oz)	1 U.S. pint
¼ pint (pt)	5 fluid ounces
1 pint (pt)	20 fluid ounces

Metric Conversion Table

1 oz — 29 gms
2 oz — 58 gms
4 oz — 115 gms
8 oz — 230 gms
12 oz — 345 gms
1 lb — 460 gms
2.2 lbs — 1 kilogram

4 fl oz — 100 millilitres (ml)
9 fl oz — ¼ litre (250 ml)
18 fl oz — ½ litre (500 ml)
1¾ pint — 1 litre

Recipes

Here is a collection of my favourite bean recipes which I hope you will enjoy too. The quantities stated will be sufficient for four people.

I have tried to make the recipes easy to follow and they use a wide range of ingredients. Everyone has a different palate, so don't be afraid to adjust the ingredients to suit your own likes and dislikes. It is seldom necessary to follow a recipe measure for measure, and an additional vegetable or generous spoonful of your favourite herb can only improve the dish if it makes you enjoy the meal even more.

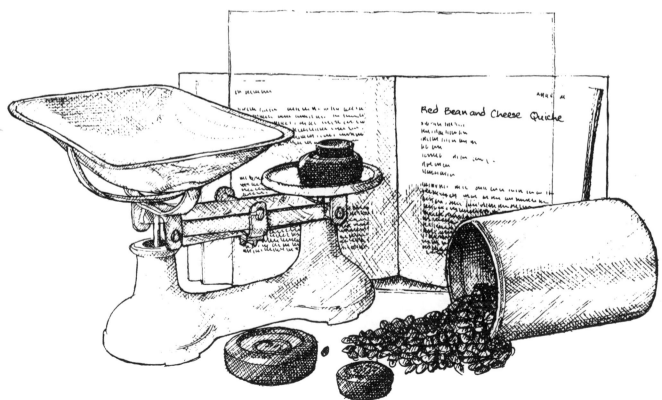

Pâtés, Spreads and Sandwich Fillings

TOFU SPREADS

Tofu is a very versatile food. Here it is used to make light, nourishing spreads that can be prepared in a moment.

Tofu Nut Spread

2 tablespoons crunchy peanut butter
2 tablespoons tofu

Mix the ingredients together to make a delicious sandwich spread.

Tofu Scrambled Eggs

2 eggs
4 tablespoons tofu
½ oz butter
seasoning

Mash the tofu and mix with the beaten eggs. Season well and cook in a pan with the melted butter. Serve on wholewheat toast.

Tofu Garbanzo Pâté

4 oz (½ cup) chick peas, soaked and drained
1 pt (2½ cups) water

Cook the beans until soft. Drain and mash well.

4 tablespoons tofu
2 tablespoons yoghurt
1 tablespoon lemon juice
½ teaspoon oregano
½ teaspoon basil
seasoning

Combine all the ingredients and adjust the seasoning to taste. Add a little extra natural yoghurt if the mixture is too stiff. Place in a dish and garnish.
   Serve with toast fingers and a light salad or as a sandwich spread.

MISO SPREADS

Some appetising and easy ways to use this excellent 'complete' protein food.

Miso and Spring Onion Spread

5 spring onions, finely chopped
4 tablespoons tahini
1 tablespoon miso
1 tablespoon soya sauce

Mix all the ingredients together and use as a sandwich filling. Garnish with crunchy beansprouts.

Miso and Orange Spread

3 tablespoons tahini
1 tablespoon miso
2-3 teaspoons orange juice
zest of 1 large orange

Combine all the ingredients. Spread on dark rye bread.

Miso and Banana Spread

3 tablespoons tahini
1 tablespoon miso
½ ripe banana

Combine all the ingredients and serve as a sandwich filling.

Miso and Cheese Spread

4 oz (1 cup) grated cheese
1½-2 teaspoons miso
½ teaspoon cider vinegar
¼ teaspoon dry mustard

Mix the ingredients together and place on slices of buttered bread. Toast until the top is golden brown and bubbly. Serve hot.

Pâté Minute

A pâté that is very simple to make. It can be used in place of cheese in sandwiches, salads and with biscuits.

8 oz (2½ cups) soya flour
8 oz (1 cup) butter
1-2 teaspoons yeast extract
pinch of paprika

Melt the butter in a pan. Remove from the heat and stir in the soya flour. Season to taste with the yeast extract and paprika. Place in a pot and leave to cool.

Soft Soya Cheese

8 oz (2½ cups) soya flour
1½ pts (3¾ cups) water
juice of 2 lemons

Blend together the flour and water and bring to the boil. Cook gently for several minutes and stir in the lemon juice. Leave to cool. Pour into a muslin cheese bag and hang above a bowl. Next day remove from the cloth and season the cheese with salt, pepper, garlic and herbs or sweeten with pineapple cubes.

Soya Pâté

4 oz (½ cup) soya beans, soaked and drained
1 pt (2½ cups) water

Cook the beans until tender. Drain.

1 onion
1 stick of celery
1½-2 tablespoons tomato purée
1 tablespoon soya oil
1 teaspoon soya sauce
½ teaspoon basil
½ teaspoon oregano

Chop the vegetables finely and sauté gently in the oil until soft. Rub the cooked beans through a sieve and discard the skins. Combine all the ingredients and season to taste. Place in a small dish and leave to cool.

Serve with toast fingers and a side salad or use as a filling for savoury pancakes.

Hummus

Hummus is a Middle Eastern dish traditionally eaten as a dip with chunks of bread and olives. It is easy to prepare and most people find it delicious.

8 oz (1 cup) chick peas, soaked and drained
2 pts (5 cups) water

Cook the beans until soft. Drain and reserve the bean stock. Mash the beans, rub them through a sieve and discard the skins. This gives the hummus a lovely smooth and light texture.

1 clove of garlic
5 tablespoons tahini
2 tablespoons natural yoghurt
juice of 3 lemons
a little bean stock
1 tablespoon olive oil
seasoning

Add the yoghurt and a little bean stock to the puréed beans until they have the same consistency as double cream. Crush the garlic and stir into the mixture. Add alternatively a little tahini and lemon juice, beating in each amount until blended. When they have both been added season to taste and adjust the consistency of the hummus by stirring in extra bean stock if necessary. Spoon the thick, creamy mixture into a flat dish and pour the olive oil over the top.

Serve with hot pitta bread as an hors d'oeuvre or a light supper dish.

Haricot and Aubergine Pâté

4 oz (½ cup) haricot beans, soaked and drained
½ pt (1¼ cups) water

Cook the beans until tender. Drain and mash them well. Rub the purée through a sieve and remove the bean skins.

1 large aubergine
2 tablespoons mayonnaise
1-2 tablespoons sour cream
2 tablespoons fresh chives, chopped
1 teaspoon lemon juice
seasoning
garnish: 1 tablespoon sesame seeds

Wrap the aubergine in foil and bake in a moderate oven for 1 hour or until soft. When cool remove the skin and mix with the haricot beans. Combine the mayonnaise, sour cream, lemon juice and chives and stir into the mixture. Season to taste.

Place the sesame seeds in a dry pan and heat through, stirring continuously, until golden brown. Remove from the pan immediately and sprinkle over the pâté. Chill before using.

Serve with a mixed green salad, corn bread and wedges of tomato and cucumber.

Butter Bean, Mushroom and Cheese Spread

An excellent snack for lunch, tea or even a late breakfast.

4 oz (½ cup) butter beans, soaked and drained
1 pt (2½ cups) water

Cook the beans until tender. Drain and reserve the bean stock. Rub the cooked beans through a sieve and discard the skins.

4 oz (1½ cups) mushrooms
3 spring onions
1 tablespoon sunflower oil
1 teaspoon soya sauce
a little bean stock
seasoning
garnish: 2 oz (½ cup) grated cheese

Slice the vegetables and fry in the oil for 5 minutes. Combine all the ingredients and adjust the seasoning to taste. Pour in a little bean stock if the mixture is too stiff. Spread on slices of bread and sprinkle the grated cheese over the top. Heat under a grill until the cheese is golden brown and bubbly.

Lentil and Sesame Pâté

Pâtés made with brown lentils have a 'meaty' texture and colour that makes them popular with everyone.

8 oz (1 cup) brown lentils
1½ pts (3¾ cups) water
1 bay leaf

Simmer the beans with the bay leaf until very soft or pressure cook them for 12 minutes. Drain the cooked beans and rub through a sieve.

8 oz (3 cups) mushrooms
2 oz (¼ cup) butter
2 onions
1 clove of garlic
2 tablespoons fresh parsley, chopped
2 teaspoons mint
3-4 teaspoons tahini
juice of 2 lemons
seasoning
garnish: 2 tablespoons melted butter

Chop the vegetables finely. Sauté the garlic and onions in butter until soft. Add the mushrooms and cook for a further 3-4 minutes. Combine all the ingredients and adjust the seasoning to taste. Press down into a pâté pot and pour over the melted butter. Garnish the dish with a bay leaf and a thin slice of mushroom. Leave to cool.

Serve with toasted wholewheat fingers and a salad consisting of tomatoes, apple and watercress.

Salads

BEAN SALADS

Beans taste just as good when served cold with
salad ingredients as they do when eaten in
piping hot winter dishes.   The key to successful
bean salads is to cook the bean just to the point
of tenderness. When making stews and casseroles
it really does not matter if the bean becomes too
soft and bursts out of its skin, it may even
improve the dish, thickening and adding flavour
to the stock. Unfortunately this does not apply to
salad dishes, whose appearance and texture may
be spoiled if the beans disintegrate when tossed
with other ingredients.

The 'perfect' salad bean must be tender but
still retain its shape. This is not always easy,
particularly when using a pressure cooker. A
useful tip is to reduce the pressure cooking time
by 2-3 minutes. Then, either reduce the pressure
gradually during which time the bean will
become tender or bring the pressure down
quickly, remove the lid and gently simmer for 5-
10 minutes until the beans are cooked.

It is easier to check the progress of beans
cooked in a pan of boiling water. All that is
needed is to test them frequently towards the
end of the cooking period.

Vinaigrette Green Beans

8 oz (1 cup) flageolet beans, soaked and drained
1 pt (2½ cups) water

Cook the beans until tender. Drain.

1 green pepper
1 mild onion
1 small lettuce
dressing:
4 tablespoons olive oil
1 tablespoon lemon juice
1 tablespoon white wine
seasoning
garnish: 1 tablespoon chopped parsley

Thinly slice the pepper and onion and mix with
the cooked beans. Combine the dressing
ingredients and pour over the beans and
vegetables. Wash the lettuce and place in the
bottom of a salad bowl. Spoon the bean mixture
over the top.

Serve with a rice salad, tomato wedges and
black olives.

Spicy Red Rosecocoes

8 oz (1 cup) rosecoco beans, soaked and
drained
1 pt (2½ cups) water

Cook the beans until tender. Drain.

1 medium lettuce
½ lb young spinach leaves
½ cucumber, sliced
1 mild onion, sliced
3 sticks of celery, sliced

dressing:
5 tablespoons tomato juice
1 tablespoon sunflower oil
1 tablespoon lemon juice
1 clove of garlic, crushed
½ teaspoon paprika

Wash and trim the lettuce and spinach. Tear into small pieces and put into a salad bowl with the beans, onion, cucumber and celery. Whisk the dressing ingredients together until smooth. Pour over the salad greens and serve immediately.

Serve with pancake rolls and a salad niçoise.

Turkish Salad

8 oz (1 cup) haricot beans, soaked and drained
1 pt (2½ cups) water

Cook the beans until tender. Drain.

3 tomatoes, sliced
5 spring onions, chopped
1 tablespoon fresh parsley, chopped
1 tablespoon fresh mint, chopped
dressing:
4 tablespoons olive oil
2 tablespoons lemon juice
seasoning

Blend the olive oil and lemon juice together and season well. Mix the cooked beans with the herbs, tomatoes and spring onions. Marinate in the dressing.

Serve with a bowl of couscous and a salad of cauliflower, courgettes and mushrooms.

Russian Red Beans

A crunchy salad with a sensational pink-coloured dressing.

8 oz (1 cup) red kidney beans, soaked and drained
1 pt (2½ cups) water

Cook the beans until tender. Drain.

dressing:
2 medium raw beetroots
1 mild onion
5 tablespoons sour cream/natural yoghurt
½ teaspoon caraway seeds

Grate the beetroot, slice the onion and mix with the cooked beans. Toss in the sour cream or yoghurt and sprinkle with the caraway seeds.

Serve with french fried potatoes and a green salad.

Blackeye Beans and Tomatoes

8 oz (1 cup) blackeye beans, soaked and drained
1 pt (2½ cups) water

Cook the beans until tender. Drain.

4 tomatoes
½ cucumber
6 spring onions
dressing:
2 tablespoons safflower oil
1 tablespoon wine vinegar
½ teaspoon dry mustard
seasoning

Chop the vegetables and mix with the cooked beans. Blend together the oil, vinegar, mustard and seasoning. Toss with the other ingredients just before serving.

Serve on a bed of lettuce with a bowl of green beans, mushrooms and sweetcorn.

Chick Pea Coleslaw

A lighter dressing, with fewer calories, can be made from a mixture of mayonnaise and yoghurt.

4 oz (½ cup) chick peas, soaked and drained
1 pt (2½ cups) water

Cook the beans until tender. Drain.

½ small white cabbage, shredded
8 oz (2 cups) carrot, grated
6 oz (1cup) mild onions, sliced
dressing:
5 tablespoons mayonnaise
seasoning

Mix the vegetables and the beans together and toss in the mayonnaise. Season to taste.

Serve with wholewheat rolls and a green salad.

Canellini Beans in a Herb Dressing

8 oz (1 cup) canellini beans, soaked and drained
1 pt (2½ cups) water
1 bay leaf

Cook the beans with the bay leaf until tender. Drain.

dressing:
3 tablespoons olive oil
1 tablespoon cider vinegar
1 teaspoon basil
1 teaspoon marjoram
seasoning

Mix the dressing ingredients together and pour over the beans.

Serve with hot garlic bread and a selection of fresh vegetables.

Garlic Bread

A french loaf
4 oz (½ cup) butter
3-4 cloves of garlic

Slice the loaf diagonally in 5-6 places, being careful not to cut through the bottom crust. Soften the butter in a pan and add the crushed garlic. Spread the garlic butter on both sides of the slices of bread and then press the loaf together. Wrap it in aluminium foil and bake in a hot oven for 45 minutes or until the loaf is crisp and golden brown in colour.

Pink Bean Platter

8 oz (1 cup) pinto beans, soaked and drained
1 pt (2½ cups) water

Cook the beans until tender. Drain.

dressing:
2 tablespoons olive oil
2 teaspoons soya oil
1 tablespoon lemon juice
1 teaspoon rosemary
garnish: 1 tablespoon fresh rosemary, chopped

Mix the salad dressing ingredients together and pour over the cooked beans while they are still hot. Leave to marinate for one hour before placing in a salad bowl and garnishing with the fresh rosemary.
 Serve with rice balls and mixed salad.

Butter Bean Salad

8 oz (1 cup) baby butter beans, soaked and drained
2 pts (5 cups) water
2 onions
1 bay leaf

Cook the beans in a pot with the peeled, whole onions and the bay leaf. Drain and remove the bay leaf.

dressing:
4 tablespoons fresh parsley, chopped
1 teaspoon thyme
1 teaspoon marjoram
juice of 1 lemon
seasoning

Mince the onions when cool and combine all the ingredients. Adjust the seasoning to taste.
 Serve with a colourful rice salad and a selection of vegetables.

BEAN SPROUT SALADS

A basic salad can be turned into an unusual and nutritious meal simply by adding a small quantity of bean sprouts. Although the most common bean sprout is grown from the mung bean any type of pulse can be used in these recipes.

Bean Sprout Waldorf

8 oz (2 cups) bean sprouts
4 sticks of celery
3 crisp, red apples
2 oz (½ cup) walnuts
dressing:
⅓ pt (1 cup) natural yoghurt
1 teaspoon lemon juice
1 tablespoon fresh mint, chopped
seasoning

Chop the apples, celery and walnuts and mix with the bean sprouts. Season with freshly ground black pepper, salt and lemon juice. Stir in the yoghurt and sprinkle the top with the mint.

Serve with a rice salad and a dish of tomatoes and green peppers.

Plat de Provence

A goat's milk cheese is an excellent choice for this salad. Its 'tangy' flavour provides a perfect contrast to the sweetness of the black grapes.

8 oz (2 cups) bean sprouts
½ lb black grapes
½ lb small courgettes
4 oz (1 cup) crumbly white cheese
dressing:
2 tablespoons olive oil
1 tablespoon wine vinegar
seasoning

Halve the grapes and remove any pips. Slice the courgettes and mix with the beansprouts, grapes and cheese. Combine the dressing ingredients together and toss with the vegetables.

Serve with french bread, salted tomatoes and olives. A dish of fresh figs could follow the meal.

Wheat Berry Salad

4 oz (1 cup) bean sprouts
½ cauliflower, lightly steamed
1 yellow pepper, sliced
4 oz (½ cup) cooked wheat
dressing:
3 tablespoons tahini
3 tablespoons natural yoghurt
2 tablespoons lemon juice
seasoning

To cook the wheat berries, first lightly roast in a dry pan until they begin to darken and smell deliciously nutty. Remove from the pan while adding ¾ pt (2 cups) of water. Bring to the boil, add the roasted wheat and simmer gently for 1-1½ hours. Drain.

Mix the bean sprouts, cauliflower florets, yellow pepper and wheat together. Beat the dressing ingredients together until well blended and pour over the salad.

Serve with buttered carrots seasoned with thyme and a mixed green salad.

Oriental Salad

The use of soya sauce in Chinese and Japanese cooking is ubiquitous and the salad dressing is no exception. The sauce has a distinct flavour that enhances, rather than overwhelms, tender salad vegetables.

8 oz (2 cups) bean sprouts
8 oz (2 cups) chinese leaves
4 oz (1½ cups) mushrooms
½ cucumber
dressing:
3 tablespoons sesame oil
1½ tablespoons soya sauce
pinch of paprika

Wash and shred the chinese leaves and lay in the bottom of a salad bowl. Slice the cucumber and mushrooms and mix with the bean sprouts. Blend the oil, soya sauce and paprika together and pour over the vegetables. Toss the ingredients together before placing in the salad bowl.

Serve with rice and stir-fry carrots, lightly garnished with sesame seeds.

TOFU SALADS

Tofu, or bean curd is an excellent source of
'complete' protein and is both easy to digest and
low in calories. It can be used whole, in bite
sized pieces, or blended with other ingredients.

Melon Medley

½ melon
4 pears
1 head of chicory
dressing:
4 tablespoons tofu
1 tablespoon sunflower oil
2 teaspoons lemon juice
seasoning
garnish: 2 tablespoons sunflower seeds

Dry roast the sunflower seeds in a pan until they
are golden in colour and smell deliciously nutty.

Trim the fruit and cut into small chunks. Blend
the tofu, oil and lemon juice together until
smooth and creamy. Season to taste. Toss the
fruit in the dressing and place in a salad bowl
lined with chicory leaves. Sprinkle with the
toasted sunflower seeds before serving.

Eat as a starter, side dish or with other salads.

Tangerine Tofu

It is best to use a non-stick or well oiled cast iron
frying pan for this recipe.

8 oz (1 cup) tofu
2 tangerines
2 slices of wholewheat bread
lettuce heart
1 box of mustard and cress
2 tablespoons sesame oil
1 tablespoon lemon juice
seasoning

Cut the tofu and the bread into 1 inch cubes.
First gently fry the tofu in a little of the sesame
oil until golden brown and crisp on the outside.
Place on a kitchen towel to drain. Sprinkle with
the lemon juice and freshly ground black pepper
while hot. Fry the bread in the remaining oil.
Shred the lettuce and mix with the cress and
tangerine segments. Lightly toss in the tofu and
croûtons before placing in a salad bowl.

Serve as a starter or with a dish of chinese
vegetables.

Soups

Farmhouse Pottage

A thick, warming soup that is almost a meal in itself.

8 oz (1 cup) brown lentils
2 pts (5 cups) water
4 oz (1 cup) white turnip, chopped
4 oz (1 cup) carrots, chopped
2 sticks of celery
1 leek
4 oz (1½ cups) mushrooms
3 tomatoes
1 parsnip
2 oz (¼ cup) cooked brown rice
½ teaspoon mustard
1 bay leaf
1 teaspoon yeast extract
2 teaspoons soya sauce
a little sunflower oil

Chop all the vegetables and sauté for several minutes in the oil. Combine all the ingredients and simmer for 1-1½ hours or pressure cook for 10 minutes. Dilute and/or blend to desired consistency and season to taste.
    Serve with wholewheat dumplings.

Dumplings

2 eggs, beaten
2 oz (½ cup) wholewheat flour
6 tablespoons butter
seasoning

Soften the butter in a pan. Mix in the flour and gradually add the beaten eggs. Season well. Drop the mixture, teaspoon by teaspoon, into the gently boiling soup and, when the dumplings have risen to the surface, cook for 5 minutes.

Minestrone Soup

In Italy minestrone soup is served before the evening meal. It is, however, a very substantial soup and may be served as a light lunch or supper dish. To make it more authentic it can be garnished with 'pesto', a sauce consisting of basil, oil, pine kernels and cheese. A more modest version can be made by pounding 2 tablespoons of freshly grated parmesan cheese with an equivalent amount of basil, 1 tablespoon of olive oil and a crushed garlic clove. 'Pesto' should be stirred into the soup just before serving.

4 oz (½ cup) haricot beans, soaked and drained
½ pt (1¼ cups) water
1 bay leaf

Cook the beans with the bay leaf until tender. Drain and reserve the bean stock.

8 oz (1 cup) tomatoes, chopped
4 oz (1 cup) white cabbage, shredded
1 onion
1 leek
2 sticks of celery
2 oz (½ cup) green beans
2 oz (½ cup) garden peas
4 oz (½ cup) wholewheat pasta
4 tablespoons fresh parsley, chopped
3 tablespoons olive oil
1 teaspoon oregano
2½ pts (6¼ cups) stock/water
freshly ground black pepper

Chop the onion, celery, leek and white cabbage and fry gently in the olive oil for 5 minutes. Add the oregano, chopped tomatoes and the liquid. Bring to the boil and simmer gently for 15 minutes. Mix in the peas, green beans, cooked beans and the pasta and simmer until the pasta is soft. Season with the chopped parsley and freshly ground black pepper.
Serve with crusty bread rolls, 'pesto' and a carafe of red wine.

Chick Pea Soup with Pasta

8 oz (1 cup) chick peas, soaked and drained
2 pts (5 cups) water

Cook the beans until tender. Drain and reserve the bean stock.

8 oz (1 cup) tomatoes, sliced
3 oz (½ cup) wholewheat macaroni
1 onion
1 tablespoon olive oil
1 tablespoon tomato purée
1 teaspoon soya sauce
1 teaspoon rosemary
1¾ pts (4½ cups) bean stock/water
seasoning

Chop the onion and sauté lightly in the olive oil. Stir in the sliced tomatoes, tomato purée, soya sauce, rosemary, the beans and stock. Bring to the boil and add the pasta. Simmer gently until it is cooked. Season well and adjust the consistency if necessary.
Serve as a main course dish with pitta bread and a fresh green salad.

Mulligatawny Soup

Here is a classic eastern soup in which the musty flavour of the yellow split peas blends perfectly with the spicy seasoning. The lemon juice gives the soup an extra 'bite' and enhances the other flavours. It is a really warming soup, ideal for winter evenings.

8 oz (1 cup) yellow split peas
2 pts (5 cups) stock/water
1 large onion
1 clove of garlic
1 parsnip
1 bay leaf
1 dessertspoon curry powder
1 teaspoon garam masala
1 green chilli (optional)
1 tablespoon soya sauce
1 tablespoon lemon juice
1 tablespoon olive oil
4 peppercorns

Finely chop the vegetables and sauté lightly in the olive oil. Mix in the spices and cook for a few minutes more, stirring constantly. Slowly pour in the stock or water and then the yellow split peas. Add the peppercorns and bay leaf and bring to the boil. Simmer gently for 1 hour or pressure cook for 10 minutes. When the beans have reduced to a purée, remove the bay leaf and season with the lemon juice and soya sauce. Beat lightly with a fork to give a light, smooth texture.
   Serve with 'nan', a kind of unleavened bread.

Nan

1 lb (4 cups) wholewheat flour
3 tablespoons ghee/oil
½ pt (1¼ cups) milk
½ teaspoon salt

Preheat the oven to 350°F/180°C/Reg 4. Mix the ghee, flour and salt together and add sufficient milk to form a soft dough. Knead until the dough becomes pliant and roll out in 4 inch diameter circles, ½ inch thick. Bake on a greased tray for 20-25 minutes.
   Serve hot.

Miso Soup

A traditional Japanese dish that is highly nutritious and very easy to digest. It is an excellent soup to give to convalescents.

¼ small white cabbage, shredded
1 onion
1 leek

1 carrot
1 clove of garlic
2 tablespoons sesame oil
1 tablespoon miso
1½ pts (3¾ cups) stock/water

Chop the vegetables and lightly fry in the oil.
Pour in the stock and bring to the boil. Simmer
gently for 15-20 minutes or until the vegetables
are tender. Blend the miso with 1 tablespoon of
cold water and pour into the soup.

Serve with buckwheat noodles.

Be careful not to boil the soup after the miso
has been added as this destroys much of its
food value.

Butter Bean and Carrot Soup

This lovely, pale golden soup has a smooth
consistency and is very nourishing. It is good
served with crispy fried croûtons.

4 oz (½ cup) butter beans, soaked and drained
1 pt (2½ cups) water

Cook the beans until soft. Drain and reserve the
bean stock.

1 lb (4 cups) carrots, sliced
2 large potatoes
1 tablespoon butter
¾ pt (2 cups) bean stock
¾ pt (2 cups) milk
1-2 teaspoons thyme
seasoning

croûtons:
3 slices of wholewheat bread
1 egg, beaten
3 tablespoons sesame seeds
1 tablespoon sesame oil

Slice the carrots and potatoes and sauté in the
butter for 10 minutes. Add the cooked beans,
bean stock, milk and thyme. Bring to the boil
and cook until the vegetables are soft. Blend to a
purée. Adjust the seasoning and consistency to
taste. Pour into a soup tureen.

To make the croûtons, cut the bread into 1
inch squares and dip in the beaten egg. Coat
them with the sesame seeds and fry on both
sides.

Drop the croûtons on top of the soup
immediately before serving.

Chestnut Soup

This is an unusual soup with a distinctive flavour.
It has a rich, creamy texture and is very filling.

4 oz (½ cup) canellini beans, soaked and drained
½ pt (1¼ cups) water

Cook the beans until tender. Drain and reserve
the stock.

1 lb chestnuts
1 stick of celery
1 onion
1 tablespoon butter
1½ pts (3¾ cups) water
seasoning

Slit the chestnuts with a knife and bake in a moderate oven until soft. When cool, remove the shells and skins.

Chop the vegetables and soften in the butter. Mix in the beans, chestnuts and water and blend to a purée. Season well and dilute with a little milk to the desired consistency. Heat thoroughly.

Serve with warm french bread.

Cream of Lentil Soup

8 oz (1 cup) red lentils
2 pts (5 cups) water
2 sticks of celery
2 large carrots
2 onions
1 clove of garlic
2 tablespoons soya sauce
2 tablespoons safflower oil
seasoning

Chop the vegetables and sauté gently in the oil. Combine all the ingredients and simmer for 45 minutes, or pressure cook for 8 minutes. Blend the soup to make it thick and creamy and adjust the seasoning to taste.

Serve with pancake rolls and a crisp green salad for lunch.

Leek and Green Pea Purée

8 oz (1 cup) green split peas
3 medium leeks
1 clove of garlic
1 onion
2 bay leaves
1 teaspoon dill seeds
1 teaspoon savory
1 tablespoon olive oil
juice of ½ lemon
2 pts (5 cups) stock/water
seasoning

Finely chop the onion and garlic and sauté in the oil for a few minutes. Trim and slice the leaks and combine all the ingredients *except for* the lemon juice. Cover the pan and simmer for 1 hour or pressure cook for 10 minutes. When cooked remove the bay leaves and season with the lemon juice, salt and pepper. Blend to a creamy consistency. Garnish with thin slices of lemon.

Serve with garlic bread.

Curried Lentil Soup

8 oz (1 cup) red lentils
2 pts (5 cups) water
1 tablespoon butter
1 tablespoon brown rice
1 onion
1 clove of garlic
2 teaspoons curry powder
¼ teaspoon cinnamon
¼ teaspoon chilli powder
juice of 1 lemon
2 tablespoons fresh coriander/parsley
seasoning

Chop the onion and garlic and sauté for a few minutes in the butter. Stir in the spices and add the rice, lentils and water. Bring to the boil and simmer for 45 minutes or pressure cook for 8 minutes. Season with the lemon juice, salt and pepper. Sprinkle the top of the soup with the chopped coriander or parsley.

Serve with warm chapatti bread and an onion raita.

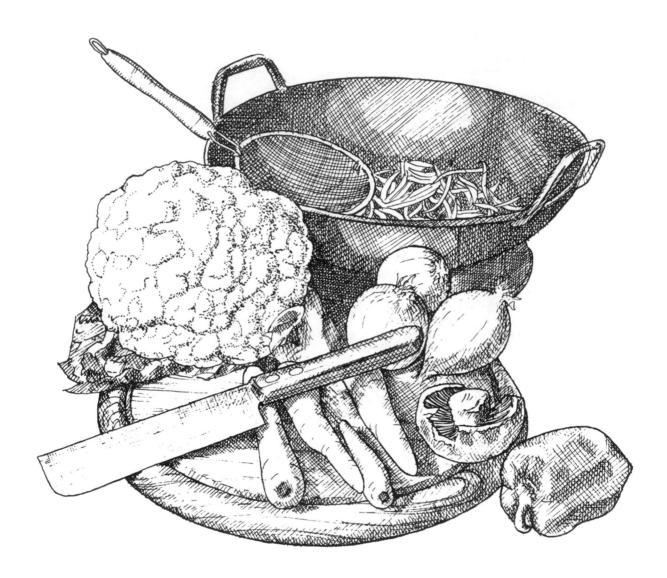

Stove-Top Dishes

Lentil and Cheese Rissoles

A quick and easy dish to prepare and one that is low in fat and high in protein.

6 oz (¾ cup) red lentils
¾ pt (2 cups) water

Cook until soft. Drain and mash well.

4 oz (½ cup) cottage cheese
5 spring onions
2 oz (½ cup) fresh wholewheat breadcrumbs
1 teaspoon thyme
seasoning
To coat:
1 oz (½ cup) wheatgerm

Chop the spring onions finely and combine with the other ingredients. Season to taste. Roll out into sausage shapes and coat in the wheatgerm. Leave in a cool place for ½ hour to become firm. Fry in a little oil until golden brown or place on a greased baking tray and cook in an oven heated to 350°F/180°C/Reg 4 for 20 minutes.

Mung Beans Cooked in Yoghurt

Yoghurt is often served with hot foods to help soften the impact of the spices on the taste buds and the digestive system. Nonetheless this curry may still be a little hot to the uninitiated! If in doubt reduce the amount of spices stated in the recipe.

4 oz (½ cup) mung beans, soaked and drained
½ pt (1¼ cups) water

Cook the beans until tender. Drain.

1 lb (3¼ cups) new potatoes, cooked
½ lb (1 cup) tomatoes, peeled and chopped
½ pt (1¼ cups) natural yoghurt
4 tablespoons raisins
3 tablespoons butter
1 onion
1 inch fresh root ginger
1 teaspoon turmeric
1 teaspoon ground coriander
1 teaspoon cumin
½ fresh green chilli
¼ teaspoon ground mace
garnish: 1 tablespoon fresh coriander leaves, chopped

Heat the butter in a large frying pan and sauté the finely chopped onion and ginger until soft and golden. Stir in the ground coriander, turmeric, cumin and chopped chilli and cook for a further 3-4 minutes. Add the tomatoes and yoghurt and simmer gently until the sauce begins to thicken. Mix with the potatoes, beans, mace and raisins and heat through.

Sprinkle the fresh coriander over the top and serve with chapatties and a sweet chutney.

Samosas

A traditional Indian food similar to pakoras, fritters and tempura. Samosas are small, triangular shaped pastry cases filled with vegetables and deep fried until crisp and golden on the outside. They can be eaten hot or cold —

Chapatties

An unleavened wheat bread in the form of round, flat rolls about 6 inches in diameter. They are traditionally served with hot, spicy foods as an alternative to rice. Indians use them for wrapping round and picking up pieces of food instead of using western cutlery; the difference being that you eat your 'cutlery' too! Chapatties are easy to make although frozen varieties are now on sale in many stores and supermarkets. To cook them you need a heavy, thick frying pan and a very small amount of butter.

8 oz (1 cup) wholewheat flour
1 teaspoon salt
¼ pt (½ cup) water

Mix the flour, salt and water together to form a dough. Knead well until it becomes soft and pliant. Set aside in a warm place for 30 minutes. Divide the mixture into 10 pieces and roll out into thin circles. Lightly grease the frying pan and heat well. Cook the chapatties one at a time until the surface begins to bubble and turn brown. Turn over and cook the under side. Store the chapatties on top of each other until the mixture is used up and the meal is about to be served. Wrap them in a cloth to keep in the heat.

on picnics, as hors d'oeuvres or as a snack with a cucumber and mint raita.

pastry:
3 tablespoons butter/ghee
4 oz (1 cup) unbleached white flour
2 oz (½ cup) chick pea flour
¼ pt (½ cup) natural yoghurt

filling:
6 cooked potatoes, diced
3 oz (½ cup) fresh green peas
1 onion
1 tablespoon fresh coriander, chopped
1 tablespoon lemon juice
1 tablespoon butter/ghee
1 teaspoon garam masala
½ teaspoon chilli powder
¼ teaspoon turmeric
seasoning

To make the pastry first rub the butter or ghee into the flours until it resembles breadcrumbs. Gradually add the yoghurt and knead it into a smooth dough. Leave in a cool place for 20-25 minutes.

Chop the onion and soften in the remaining butter/ghee. Mix in all the other filling ingredients and cook gently until the mixture becomes a little dry. Leave to cool.

Roll out the pastry very thinly and cut into 2 inch squares. Put 1-2 tablespoons of the filling mixture into the centre of each pastry square. Moisten the pastry edges with water before folding over to form a triangle. Press the edges together and fry until golden brown.

Cucumber and Mint Raita

Thinly dice a 3 inch piece of cucumber and stir into a small bowl of natural yoghurt. Season well with freshly chopped mint and serve as a dip or sauce.

Tomato and Soya Hotpot

8 oz (1 cup) soya beans, soaked and drained
2 pts (5 cups) water

Cook the beans until tender. Drain and reserve the stock.

¾ lb (1½ cups) tomatoes, peeled and chopped
2 onions
2 sticks of celery
1 green pepper
2 tablespoons soya flour
1 tablespoon soya sauce
1 tablespoon olive oil
1¼ pts (3¼ cups) bean stock
1 teaspoon basil
½ teaspoon oregano
½ teaspoon cayenne

Chop the vegetables and sauté the onion, celery and pepper in the oil until they begin to soften. Add the tomatoes and cook for a further 5 minutes. Stir in the flour and gradually add the bean stock. Mix in the beans and the herbs and simmer in a covered pot for 15 minutes. Season with soya sauce.

Serve with a bowl of brown rice and a green vegetable.

Bean Burgers

A useful way of using up leftover beans. Be sure to make the mixture moist to ensure that the burgers hold together during cooking and are mouth-watering when eaten.

8 oz (1 cup) black beans, soaked and drained
2 pts (5 cups) water

Cook the beans until tender. Drain and mash half the quantity only.

2 large onions
2 oz (⅔ cup) buckwheat flour
1 tablespoon soya sauce
1-2 teaspoons sage
1 tablespoon soya oil

Grate the onions and sauté lightly in the oil until soft. Combine all the ingredients together and leave in a cool place for ½ hour to firm up. Divide the mixture into 8 balls and flatten in the hand to form small cakes. Fry over a moderate heat or bake in an oven until they are heated through and golden brown on the outside.

    Serve with fried apple rings and a carrot and potato purée.

Black Beans in a Cream Sauce

8 oz (1 cup) black beans, soaked and drained
1 pt (2½ cups) water

Cook the beans until tender. Drain.

8 oz (3 cups) mushrooms, chopped

2 mild onions, chopped
¼ pt (½ cup) sour cream
¼ pt (½ cup) natural yoghurt
1 tablespoon unbleached white flour
2 tablespoons butter
seasoning

Sauté the onions and mushrooms in the butter until soft. Stir in the beans and the flour. Gradually add the sour cream and the yoghurt and mix well until the sauce is smooth. Heat gently, stirring all the time, until the sauce has thickened. Be careful not to boil the ingredients as this will cause the cream and yoghurt to separate out.

Italian Bean Pot

The use of tomatoes, courgettes, pasta, basil and oregano give this dish a true Mediterranean flavour.

6 oz (¾ cup) kidney beans, soaked and drained
2 oz (¼ cup) brown lentils
1½ pts (3¾ cups) water

Cook the beans until tender. Drain and reserve the stock.

1 lb (2 cups) tomatoes, chopped
2 leeks
2 courgettes
2 sticks of celery
1 onion
8 oz (1⅓ cups) wholewheat pasta
2 tablespoons tomato purée

2 tablespoons olive oil
2 bay leaves
1 teaspoon basil
1 teaspoon oregano
¾ pt (2 cups) bean stock
seasoning

Slice the onion and celery and fry in the oil until transparent. Chop the remaining vegetables and sauté lightly for 3-5 minutes. Combine all the ingredients and simmer until the pasta is cooked.

Garnish with cheese and serve with crispy bread rolls, garlic butter and a green salad.

Pinto Beans and Spicy Apple

A sweet and sour dish that has a Caribbean flavour.

8 oz (1 cup) pinto beans, soaked and drained
1 pt (2½ cups) water
1 onion
4 cloves

Push the cloves into the onion and cook with the beans. When tender, drain and remove the cloves. Mince the onion and add to the cooked beans.

2 cooking apples
2 sticks of celery
2 oz (½ cup) raisins
2 tablespoons chopped parsley
2 teaspoons olive oil
½ teaspoon cinnamon
¼ teaspoon mace

2 teaspoons cider vinegar
seasoning

Dice the celery and sauté until soft in the olive oil. Wash, core and slice the apples and cook gently with the celery for 4-5 minutes. Mix together all the remaining ingredients and adjust the seasoning to taste.

Serve as a filling for savoury pancake rolls and accompany with a carrot, white cabbage and walnut salad in a sour cream dressing.

East Indian Garbanzos

8 oz (1 cup) chick peas, soaked and drained
2 pts (5 cups) water

Cook the beans until tender. Drain well reserving the stock.

2 onions
1 green pepper
1 tomato
½ green chilli
2 tablespoons chopped parsley/coriander
1 tablespoon olive oil
1 teaspoon turmeric
½ teaspoon cumin
½ teaspoon ground ginger
¼ pt (½ cup) bean stock

Slice the onions, chilli and pepper and sauté in a little oil. Mix in the cooked chick peas and the spices and cook over a low heat for 5-10 minutes. Chop the tomato and add to the pan with the bean stock. Simmer gently until most of the liquid has evaporated off. Sprinkle with the parsley or coriander.

Serve with a pilau rice consisting of spiced brown rice cooked with apricots and cashew nuts and a green salad. A fruit compote of fresh pineapple, persimmons, peaches and coconut flakes could complete the meal.

Bean Sprout Pilau

8 oz (2 cups) bean sprouts
8 oz (1 cup) brown rice, cooked
1 carrot, grated
1 green pepper, sliced
1 bunch of watercress, chopped
4 oz (1 cup) raisins
4 oz (1 cup) toasted sunflower seeds
3 tablespoons sunflower oil
juice of 1 lemon
seasoning

Sauté the cooked rice, carrot and green pepper in the oil and season with salt, pepper and lemon juice. Combine all the ingredients and heat through, stirring all the time.

Serve hot or cold with tomato wedges, buttered aubergines and a sour cream sauce.

Miso and Almonds

This is a really beautiful dish that is easy to prepare and never fails to impress. It is best made with cooked rice that has been allowed to cool. This ensures that the consistency does not become too moist and sticky.

8 oz (1 cup) brown rice, cooked
3 tablespoons flaked almonds
2 eggs
2 tablespoons butter
6 large spring onions
1 clove of garlic, crushed
1 dessertspoon miso
1 dessertspoon cold water

Sauté 2 tablespoons flaked almonds, the garlic and finely chopped onions in 1 tablespoon of butter. Remove from the pan when the almonds have become golden brown. Beat the eggs and lightly scramble in the remaining butter. Add the rice and cook for a further 3-4 minutes. Blend the miso with the water and stir into the mixture. Combine with the sautéed almonds and onions and adjust the seasoning to taste. Place in a serving bowl. Toast the remaining almonds to bring out their full flavour before sprinkling them on the top of the rice.

Allow to cool before serving with a selection of salad dishes.

Wheat Berry Risotto

Whole wheat featured strongly in traditional nineteenth century cooking when it was used to make filling dishes such as frumenty, a forerunner of muesli and other breakfast foods. Although it is one of the world's leading cereals it is unusual to see wheat berries on sale in the shops. More often than not the grain is milled and sold as flour, bread, biscuits and pasta. Whole wheat is a delicious grain and deserves to be used more often. It makes a pleasant alternative to brown rice and is much cheaper. There is just one disadvantage — it takes over an hour to cook and even then it will be relatively chewy. A wholewheat risotto makes a nourishing and filling meal but not one that can be bolted down in a hurry!

8 oz (1 cup) blackeye beans
1 pt (2½ cups) water

Cook until tender. Drain and reserve the bean stock.

8 oz (1⅓ cups) wheat berries
8 oz (1 cup) brussels sprouts, chopped
2 large carrots
2 leeks
1 onion
1 tablespoon safflower oil
2 teaspoons soya sauce
¼ pt (½ cup) bean stock

Lightly roast the wheat berries in a dry pan until they begin to darken in colour and smell deliciously nutty. Remove from the heat while adding 1½ pints (3¾ cups) of water. Bring to the boil, add the roasted wheat and simmer gently for 1-1½ hours. Drain.

Slice the onion and fry in the oil until soft. Chop the remaining vegetables and cook for 5 minutes with the onions. Add the soya sauce and bean stock and bring to the boil. Reduce the heat and simmer for 10-15 minutes or until the vegetables are just tender and the stock has evaporated away. Toss in the cooked beans and wheat and heat through before serving.

Eat as a light luncheon or supper dish.

Lentil Spaghetti Bolognese

The brown lentils provide colour, body and flavour to this substantial vegetarian dish.

8 oz (1 cup) brown lentils
1 pt (2½ cups) water
1 bay leaf

Place the bay leaf with the beans and cook until tender. Drain and reserve the bean stock.

8 oz (1 cup) tomatoes, peeled and chopped
4 oz (1½ cups) mushrooms
3 carrots
2 sticks of celery
2 onions
1 cooking apple
1 clove of garlic
1 tablespoon tomato purée
2 tablespoons olive oil
¾ pt (2 cups) bean stock
¼ pt (½ cup) dry cider
juice of 1 lemon
1 teaspoon oregano
seasoning

Chop the vegetables finely and sauté in the olive oil until they are soft. Combine all the remaining ingredients and bring to the boil. Simmer in a covered pan for 45 minutes. Adjust seasoning to taste.

Serve with a bowl of wholewheat spaghetti and lots of freshly grated parmesan cheese to sprinkle on the top. An Italian style side salad consisting of peppers, courgettes and olives could accompany the meal.

Chinese Vegetables

The stir fry is probably the most well known and popular aspect of Chinese cuisine. The food is cooked very quickly, in a minimum amount of oil, thus sealing in both the flavour and goodness. It is customary to use a wok but a large frying pan can be used in its place. Almost any vegetable may be used as long as it is cut into a suitable shape and size to ensure that it cooks evenly and quickly. The Chinese pay particular attention to the preparation of the vegetables. They are usually cut into small, delicate, bite sized pieces often in the shape of doves, crescents, flowers and stars.

8 oz (2 cups) bean sprouts
4 oz (¾ cup) courgettes, sliced
4 oz (1¼ cups) mushrooms
1 green pepper
3 carrots
1 inch fresh root ginger
1-2 teaspoons sesame oil
2 teaspoons soya sauce

Crush the root ginger, cut the carrots into julienne strips, the pepper into thin rings and slice the mushrooms and courgettes. Heat the oil in a wok or large pan and sauté the ginger for a few minutes. Add the green pepper and carrots and stir-fry for 5 more minutes. Toss in the mushrooms and courgettes and cook for a few minutes more. Mix in the bean sprouts and sprinkle over the soya sauce. Cover the pan and cook over a low heat for 3-4 minutes. The vegetables should be firm and slightly crunchy.

Serve with egg noodles in individual bowls and eat the meal with chopsticks. A fruit compote of pears, lychees, chinese gooseberries and tangerine segments could accompany the dish.

Tempura

Tempura simply means deep-fried food that has been previously coated in batter. Any food can be used — carrots, cauliflower, broccoli, leeks, brussels sprouts, potatoes, banana and apple are a few examples. Hard root vegetables may need to be par boiled before being coated and fried.

Achieving the correct batter consistency may require a little practice so if at first you don't succeed do try again. The batter must be sufficiently thin to allow the food underneath to cook and yet it must coat the food evenly without becoming heavy and stodgy. This may sound rather daunting but the end result is so good that it makes all the effort worthwhile. Tempura vegetables are highly nutritious as the goodness is sealed inside the crisp outer layer.

To make the batter you will need:

4 oz (1 cup) unbleached white flour
4 oz (1 cup) chick pea flour
2 eggs
⅓ pt (1 cup) milk
seasoning

Mix the flours together and gradually stir in the beaten eggs. Add the milk slowly until the consistency of the batter resembles thick cream.

Heat a pan of oil to 350°F/180°C. Dip the chopped vegetables in the batter and drop into the oil. They should rise to the surface and become golden brown in about 5 minutes. Drain off any surplus oil and serve immediately.

Tempura is served on a bed of rice with tentsuya – a dip from the Far East. To make this you will need:

¼ pt (½ cup) vegetable stock
2 tablespoons soya sauce
a little freshly grated ginger
2 tablespoons of sake

Combine all the ingredients and bring to the boil. Use as a dip or sauce.

Frijoles Refritos

Most people think of Chilli Con Carne as Mexico's national dish but you are more likely to find a Mexican eating frijoles refritos. Apparently they are eaten for breakfast, dinner, tea and supper!

8 oz (1 cup) rosecoco beans, soaked and drained
1 pt (2½ cups) water
2 teaspoons cumin seeds

Cook the beans with the cumin seeds until soft. Drain.

Mash half of the beans with a fork and mix with the whole, cooked rosecocoes. Shape into small flat patties and fry gently in a little oil until heated through.

Esau's Pottage

Esau sold his inheritance for a bowl of this thick, nourishing stew.

1½ lbs (3 cups) red lentils
2 oz (¼ cup) brown rice
2 oz (¼ cup) butter
4 pts (10 cups) water
4 onions, chopped
seasoning

Sauté the onions in the butter until soft and transparent. Add the remaining ingredients and cook until the pottage begins to thicken and the rice becomes soft. Adjust seasoning to taste before serving.

Moors and Christians

This is a popular dish in Cuba where it is eaten by the sugar and tobacco plantation workers. Traditionally it is made with polished white rice but the flavour and nutritional value are improved when cooked with brown rice.

8 oz (1 cup) black beans, soaked and drained
1 pt (2½ cups) water
1 onion, chopped
1 clove of garlic, crushed

Cook the beans with the onion and garlic until tender. Drain.

8 oz (1 cup) brown rice, cooked
1 red pepper, chopped
2 tablespoons fresh parsley, chopped

Mix all the ingredients together and heat through before serving.

Red Bean Goulash

A meal with a distinct Eastern European flavour.

8 oz (1 cup) red kidney beans, soaked and drained
2 pts (5 cups) water

Cook the beans until tender. Drain and reserve the bean stock.

2 onions
2 sticks of celery
2 potatoes
¼ small cauliflower
1 green pepper
2 tablespoons tomato purée
¼ pt (½ cup) natural yoghurt
1 tablespoon sunflower oil
2 teaspoons lemon juice
1½-2 teaspoons paprika
½ teaspoon caraway seeds
½ pt (1¼ cups) bean stock
seasoning

Slice the potatoes, celery, onions and pepper and fry in the oil. Pour in the bean stock and simmer, covered, for 15 minutes. Stir in the paprika, caraway seeds, yoghurt, tomato purée, cooked beans and the cauliflower florets. Cook for a further 20 minutes. Season with pepper and lemon juice.

Serve with new potatoes and a mixed green salad.

Chick Peas in Sesame Sauce

8 oz (1 cup) chick peas, soaked and drained
2 pts (5 cups) water

Cook the beans until tender. Drain and reserve
the bean stock.

½ lb (¾ cup) potatoes, cooked
2 carrots, cooked
1 green pepper
3 tablespoons wholewheat flour
2 tablespoons butter
1 tablespoon sesame oil
1 tablespoon tahini
1 tablespoon fresh parsley
1 teaspoon rosemary
1 teaspoon sage
2 bay leaves
¼ pt (½ cup) bean stock
¼ pt (½ cup) milk
seasoning

Slice the green pepper and cook in the butter and
oil until it softens. Blend in the flour and then
gradually add the bean stock and milk. Slowly
bring to the boil, stirring frequently until it forms a
thick sauce. Flavour with the tahini and herbs and
adjust the seasoning to taste. Add the cooked
chick peas and vegetables and heat through.

Serve over a bed of wholewheat pasta and
tender, lemon buttered spinach leaves.

Baby Butter Beans With Broccoli

8 oz (1 cup) baby butter beans, soaked and
drained
1 pt (2½ cups) water

Cook the beans until tender. Drain and reserve
the stock.

8 oz (1½ cups) broccoli, chopped
8 oz (1½ cups) sweetcorn
4 oz (1½ cups) mushrooms
¼ pt (½ cup) bean stock
2 courgettes
1 tablespoon soya sauce
1 tablespoon soya oil

Slice the mushrooms and courgettes. Heat the
oil in a large frying pan and stir-fry all the
vegetables for several minutes. Add the cooked
beans, the soya sauce and bean stock and
simmer gently in a covered pan for 5-10 minutes
or until the vegetables are tender.

Serve on a bed of buckwheat spaghetti with a
bowl of cauliflower tossed in a little butter and
saffron.

Succotash with Butter Beans

8 oz (1 cup) baby butter beans, soaked and
drained
1 pt (2½ cups) water

Cook the beans until tender. Drain and reserve
the stock.

8 oz (1⅓ cups) sweetcorn
2 green peppers, sliced
2 medium courgettes, sliced
1 tablespoon sunflower seeds
2 tablespoon sunflower oil
½ teaspoon mustard
seasoning
a little bean stock

Heat the oil in a pan and sauté the peppers and
courgettes for 3-4 minutes. Add the sweetcorn
and cook for a further 10 minutes, stirring
frequently.
    Lightly roast the sunflower seeds in a dry pan
or under the grill.
    Mix all the ingredients together and season to
taste. Heat through, adding a little bean stock if
the mixture is too dry.
    Serve on a bed of noodles or buckwheat
spaghetti.

Chilli Pink Beans

8 oz (1cup) pinto beans, soaked and drained
1 pt (2½ cups) water
1 teaspoon cumin seeds

Cook the beans until tender. Drain and reserve
the stock.

6 oz (1 cup) sweetcorn
7 oz (1 cup) tomatoes, peeled and chopped
1 large onion
1 large green pepper
¾ pt (2 cups) bean stock
2 teaspoons marjoram
½ red chilli
1 tablespoon sunflower oil
2 teaspoons soya sauce
seasoning

Chop the onion, green pepper and chilli and
sauté lightly in the oil. Add the bean stock,
marjoram, tomatoes and sweetcorn and cook for
a further 3 minutes. Mash half of the cooked
beans and mix them with the whole beans and
the soya sauce and the other ingredients. Bring to
the boil and simmer gently for 30 minutes.
Adjust seasoning to taste before serving.

Red Beans with Rice

It used to be customary in Japan to prepare this
dish on festive occasions. It was served cold, in
individual bowls with sesame seeds.

4 oz (½ cup) aduki beans
8 oz (1 cup) brown rice
1½ pts (3¾ cups) water
2 tablespoons sake
garnish: 2 tablespoons sesame seeds

Soak the beans and the rice together for at least

6 hours. Drain and steam for 1 hour or until they are soft. Place in a bowl and pour over the sake. Leave to stand until all the sake has been absorbed. Sprinkle with sesame seeds before serving.

Oven Dishes

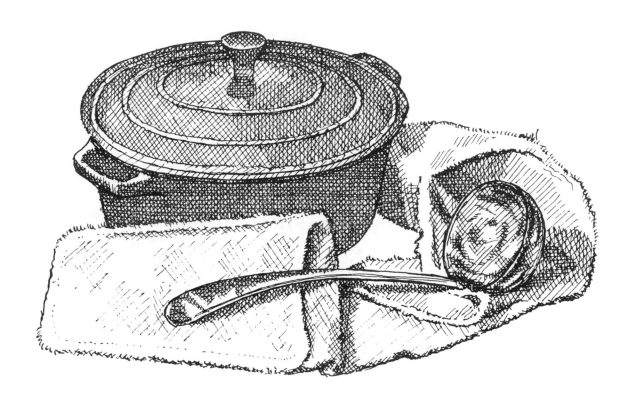

WHOLEWHEAT PASTRY

Pastry making is regarded by many as a really difficult operation, one to avoid at all costs. Certainly it is necessary to understand the meaning of such terms as to 'blind bake', 'breadcrumb consistency' and 'rubbing in' but there is no special skill needed to produce pastry.

General rules for making pastry:

1. Use a 100% plain wholewheat flour, preferably one that has been finely milled.
2. Keep everything cool and use cold water where necessary.
3. Introduce as much air as possible during the making by holding the hands above the top of the bowl while rubbing the fat into the flour.
4. Roll the pastry dough out with short, quick movements.
5. Bake at the correct temperature.

Possible problems:

1. A hard, tough pastry may be the result of adding too much liquid or handling the dough too often.

2. A crumbly pastry may be the result of using too coarse a flour or using insufficient water.

3. A rubbery, greasy pastry may be a result of cooking it at too low a temperature.

Method for making basic pastry:

1. Sieve the flour into a bowl.
2. Add the fat and rub it into the flour with the fingertips until the mixture resembles breadcrumbs. This should only take a few minutes. Cut the fat into small pieces if it hard.
3. Gradually add the cold water and mix to a stiff dough.
4. Knead lightly and roll into shape.
5. Place in a greased container.
6. Proceed as directed in the individual recipes.

Red Bean and Cheese Quiche

A 'classic' quiche that manages to be both substantial and light in texture.

4 oz (½ cup) red kidney beans, soaked and drained
½ pt (1¼ cups) water

Cook the beans until tender. Drain.

pastry:
6 oz (1½ cups) fine wholewheat flour
2 oz (¼ cup) butter
2 tablespoons sunflower oil
1 egg yolk
2 oz (½ cup) grated cheese
a little cold water
filling:
3 sticks of celery
4 eggs
1 red pepper
½ pt (1¼ cups) milk
1 tablespoon fresh, chopped parsley
1 tablespoon sunflower oil
½ teaspoon paprika
seasoning

Preheat the oven to 425°F/220°C/Reg 7.
    To make the cheese pastry rub the butter into the flour until it resembles breadcrumbs. Lightly stir in the oil, cheese and the egg yolk. Add sufficient water to give a smooth, fairly stiff dough. Roll out and line a well greased quiche dish. Prick the pastry base with a fork and blind bake in the oven for 5-8 minutes.
    Slice the vegetables and sauté in the oil until they begin to soften. Beat the eggs with the milk

and season with salt, pepper, parsley and the paprika. Put the cooked beans and vegetables into the pastry case and pour over the egg mixture. Bake for 25-30 minutes.
    Serve with a dish of new potatoes, a lettuce, cabbage, apple and tangerine salad and a carafe of red wine.

Aduki Bean and Walnut Pie

The ingredients in this pie complement the savoury/sweet quality of aduki beans. It can be served hot as part of a main meal but it also makes an excellent snack for picnics and luncheon boxes. The filling, when cooked, should be firm but moist. Be careful not to overcook the aduki beans for they soon fall away to a purée.

8 oz (1 cup) aduki beans, soaked and drained
1 pt (2½ cups) water

Cook the beans until barely tender. Drain and reserve the bean stock.

filling:
2 oz (½ cup) walnuts
2 oz (½ cup) sultanas
2 parsnips
2 leeks
1 mild onion
1 tablespoon safflower oil
1 level teaspoon cinnamon
pastry:
8 oz (2 cups) fine wholewheat flour

3 oz (⅓ cup) butter
8 teaspoons cold water
2 tablespoons sunflower oil

Preheat the oven to 400°F/200°C/Reg 6.

Grate the onion and parsnips and thinly slice the leeks. Sauté the vegetables in a little oil until they have begun to soften. Mix with the cooked beans, sultanas, walnuts and cinnamon. The mixture needs to be sticky so add a little bean stock if it is too dry.

Make the pastry and line a greased pie dish with half the amount. Spoon in the filling and top with the remaining pastry. Bake for 30-35 minutes.

Serve hot with potato cakes, an apple sauce and a green vegetable.

Butter Bean Crumble

Creamy butter beans, cheese and the mature, fruity flavour of the miso blend together to create a rich and tasty filling to this savoury crumble.

8 oz (1 cup) butter beans, soaked and drained
2 pts (5 cups) water

Cook the beans until tender. Drain and reserve the stock.

filling:
2 sticks of celery
4 carrots
2 onions
2 oz (½ cup) cheese, grated

2 tablespoons wholewheat flour
3 teaspoons miso
½ pt (1¼ cups) bean stock
1 tablespoon soya oil
topping:
2 oz (¾ cup) oat flakes
2 oz (¾ cup) porridge oats
3 tablespoons soya oil
seasoning

Preheat the oven to 400°F/200°C/Reg 6.

Dice the vegetables and fry lightly in the oil. Stir in the wholewheat flour. Blend the miso with the bean stock and gradually add to the vegetables. Mix in the cooked beans and place in a casserole. Grate the cheese over the top. Mix the topping ingredients together and sprinkle over the cheese. Bake for 30 minutes or until golden brown on the top.

Serve with a potato hotpot, braised carrots and lightly steamed kale.

Herby Bean Hotpot

8 oz (1 cup) kidney beans, soaked and drained
1 pt (2½ cups) water

Cook the beans until tender. Drain and reserve
the bean stock.

1 lb (1½ cups) potatoes, sliced
8 oz (1½ cups) courgettes, sliced
8 oz (3 cups) mushrooms
8 oz (1 cup) tomatoes, peeled and sliced
1 onion
1 green pepper
1 tablespoon olive oil
1 tablespoon butter
2 teaspoons soya sauce
2 teaspoons sage
½ pt (1¼ cups) bean stock
seasoning

Preheat the oven to 400°F/200°C/Reg 6.
    Slice the onions, pepper, courgettes and
mushrooms and sauté in the olive oil. Add the
tomatoes, cooked beans, soya sauce, sage and
bean stock and season well. Place the mixture in
a greased casserole dish and lay the sliced
potatoes on the top. Cover with aluminium foil
and bake for 45 minutes. Remove the foil and
dot the potatoes with the butter and sprinkle
with freshly ground black pepper. Cook for a
further 10 minutes or until the potatoes are
tender.
    Serve with lightly steamed green vegetables.

Indian Bean Bake

A dish with an Eastern flavour that can be eaten
hot or cold.

4 oz (½ cup) haricot beans, soaked
½ pt (1¼ cups) water

Cook the beans until tender. Drain and reserve
the stock.

1 large onion
1 large carrot
4 oz (2 cups) savoy cabbage, shredded
1 level tablespoon chopped parsley
1 level tablespoon peanut butter
1 teaspoon coriander
1 teaspoon cumin seeds
1 egg
¼ pt (½ cup) bean stock
seasoning

Preheat the oven to 350°F/180°C/Reg 4.
    Coarsely chop the vegetables. Place all the
ingredients in a blender/grinder and reduce to a
purée. Pour the mixture into a greased soufflé
dish and bake for 1 hour until it is golden brown
on top and firm to the touch.
    Serve with pitta bread, onion pakorhas and a
sweet chutney.

Onion Pakorhas

1-2 onions
4 oz (1 cup) split pea flour
½ teaspoon garam masala
½ teaspoon chilli powder
½ teaspoon turmeric
¼ teaspoon ground ginger
¼ pt (½ cup) water
oil for deep frying

Add the water to the flour until it has the consistency of thick batter. Season with the spices and beat well. Leave in a cool place for hour. Slice the onions thinly and coat with the batter. Heat the oil and deep fry until they are crisp and golden. Drain off any excess fat before serving.

Brazil Nut Roast

Millet is a delicate, yellow grain which becomes fluffy when cooked. It makes lovely light croquettes, rissoles and roasts.

6 oz (1½ cups) carrots, grated
4 oz (1 cup) ground brazil nuts
3 oz (¾ cup) millet
1 large cooking apple
1 egg
1 tablespoon miso
1 tablespoon tahini
1 teaspoon basil
1 tomato
seasoning

Preheat the oven to 375°F/190°C/Reg 5.

Dry roast the millet until it smells nutty and is golden brown in colour. Then cook in 2½ times the amount of water for 20 minutes. Drain off any remaining liquid.

Grate the apple and carrots and mix with the brazils, millet, tahini and basil. Blend 1 tablespoon of miso with 1 tablespoon of water and stir into the mixture. Season well and bind with the beaten egg. Place in a greased loaf tin and decorate with slices of tomato. Bake for 40 minutes.

Serve with a vegetable ratatouille as a savoury supper dish.

Garbanzo Nuts

8 oz (1 cup) chick peas
2 pts (5 cups) water
1-2 tablespoons soya sauce

Soak the beans in the water overnight. Drain. Preheat the oven to 350°F/180°C/Reg 4.

Toss the soaked beans in the soya sauce and leave to stand for 30 minutes. Spread the chick peas on a greased baking tray and cook for 45 minutes, turning them occasionally to ensure an even roast.

Roasted chick peas keep very well if stored in an air-tight container.

Cottage Pie

This meatless shepherd's pie lacks none of the flavour or appeal of the genuine article.

8 oz (1 cup) brown lentils
1 pt (2½ cups) water

Cook the beans until soft. Drain and reserve the stock.

1 lb (2 cups) cooked, mashed potatoes
8 oz (2 cups) grated carrot
8 oz (2 cups) grated parsnip
½ small cauliflower, trimmed
2 tablespoons yeast extract
2 tablespoons tomato purée
2 tablespoons sunflower oil
¼ pt (½ cup) bean stock
1 tablespoon butter
seasoning

Preheat the oven to 375°F/190°C/Reg 5.

Sauté the vegetables in the oil for 10 minutes before adding the cooked lentils. Cook for a further few minutes stirring frequently. Place the mixture into a casserole. Mix the yeast extract, tomato purée and bean stock together and season well. Pour the stock over the lentils and top with mashed potato. Dot with knobs of butter and bake for ½ hour.

Serve with a dish of braised vegetables, baked onions and a sweet pickle.

Devilled Haricot Beans With Leeks

8 oz (1 cup) haricot beans, soaked and drained
1 pt (2½ cups) water

Cook the beans until tender. Drain and reserve the bean stock.

3 medium leeks
2 tablespoons fresh parsley
1 tablespoon fresh thyme or 1 teaspoon dried thyme
1 bay leaf
1 clove of garlic
1 tablespoon butter
1 teaspoon mustard powder
¼ pt (½ cup) bean stock
¼ pt (½ cup) dry cider
seasoning

Preheat the oven to 400°F/200°C/Reg 6.

Wash and trim the leeks and cut into 1 inch lengths. Sauté them lightly in the butter for several minutes. Combine all the ingredients and place in a casserole. Bake for 35 minutes or until the leeks are tender.

Serve as a luncheon dish with wholewheat croûtons followed by crispy apples and salted almonds.

Sesame Soya Croquettes

Highly nutritious and an excellent way to use leftover soya beans.

4 oz (½ cup) soya beans, soaked and drained
1½ pts (3¾ cups) water

Cook the beans until tender. Drain and mash well.

1 grated onion
2 oz (½ cup) fresh wholewheat breadcrumbs
2 oz sesame seeds
4 tablespoons tahini
2 tablespoons chopped parsley
1 tablespoon soya sauce
1 tablespoon tomato purée
seasoning

Preheat the oven to 375°F/190°C/Reg 5.

Mix all the ingredients together *except for* the sesame seeds. Adjust the seasoning and consistency. Roll out into sausage shapes and coat in the sesame seeds. Place on a greased baking tray and cook in the oven for approximately 25 minutes or until the croquettes are golden brown.

Serve with potato fritters, cauliflower and a spicy tomato sauce.

Spiced Soya Beans

6 oz (¾ cup) soya beans, soaked and drained
1½ pts (3¾ cups) water

Cook the beans until tender. Drain.

2 sticks of celery
1 large onion
1 clove of garlic
2 tablespoons soya flour
1 tablespoon soya oil
2 teaspoons turmeric
1 teaspoon cumin
1 teaspoon fenugreek
½ green chilli
1 bay leaf
juice of 1 lemon
½ pt (1¼ cups) vegetable stock

Preheat the oven to 400°F/200°C/Reg 6.

Chop the vegetables and fry gently in the oil until golden brown. Stir in the soya flour and the spices. Cook gently for several minutes before adding the vegetable stock and lemon juice. Place in a casserole, cover and bake for 1 hour.

Serve on a bed of brown rice with a bowl of natural yoghurt sprinkled with coconut and cardamom seeds.

White Bean and Courgette Casserole

8 oz (1 cup) canellini beans, soaked and drained
1 pt (2½ cups) water

Cook the beans until tender. Drain and reserve the stock.

8 oz (1½ cups) courgettes, sliced
2 oz (½ cup) fresh wholewheat breadcrumbs
2 oz (½ cup) cheese, grated
½ pt (1¼ cups) bean stock
2 onions
2 large potatoes
1 clove of garlic, crushed
1 tablespoon miso
1 tablespoon sunflower oil
1 teaspoon rosemary
1 teaspoon mustard powder
seasoning

Preheat the oven to 400°F/200°C/Reg 6.
   Slice the onions and fry with the garlic until soft. Dice the potatoes and add to the onion mixture. Cook for a further 5 minutes. Blend the miso, mustard and bean stock together and add to the vegetables. Season with the rosemary and simmer gently for 10 minutes. Mix with the beans and put into a casserole. Lay the courgettes on the top and sprinkle with the grated cheese and breadcrumbs. Bake for 25-30 minutes.
   Serve with roast potatoes and brussels sprouts spiced with nutmeg. Complete the meal with a fresh fruit salad.

Blackeye Beans Cooked in Beer

This hearty stew has a lovely dark, rich gravy which enhances the flavour of the beans. It is best to use a draught beer as bottled or keg varieties do not have such a good taste.

8 oz (1 cup) blackeye beans
1 pt (2½ cups) water

Cook until tender. Drain and reserve the stock.

12 oz (3 cups) white turnip, chopped
8 oz (3 cups) mushrooms
1 large onion
¼ pt (½ cup) draught bitter beer
¼ pt (½ cup) bean stock
4 tablespoons wholewheat flour
2 tablespoons chopped parsley
2 tablespoons tomato purée
1 tablespoon sunflower oil
2 teaspoons soya sauce
½ teaspoon cinnamon
¼ teaspoon ground cloves
seasoning

Preheat the oven to 400°F/200°C/Reg 6.
   Slice the vegetables and sauté lightly in the oil. Stir in the flour and gradually blend in the bean stock. Combine all the remaining ingredients and adjust the seasoning. Bring to the boil and simmer for 5 minutes before placing in a covered casserole. Bake for 1 hour.
   Serve with jacket potatoes, baked parsnips and winter greens. A fresh fruit pie with yoghurt could accompany the meal.

Flageolet Beans au Gratin

Flageolet beans are really delicious and combine with the creamy sauce and lemon juice to make a perfect dish.

4 oz (½ cup) flageolet beans, soaked and drained
½ pt (1¼ cups) water

Cook the beans until tender. Drain.

8 oz (3 cups) mushrooms
8 oz (1 cup) buckwheat noodles
2 leeks
1 tablespoon olive oil
1 tablespoon lemon juice
1 tablespoon fresh parsley, chopped
1 tablespoon butter
1 tablespoon unbleached white flour
¼ pt (½ cup) sour cream/natural yoghurt
½ pt (1¼ cups) creamy milk
seasoning

Preheat the oven to 400°F/200°C/Reg 6.
   Cook the pasta in boiling water until soft. Trim and slice the leeks and steam for 5 minutes
   Sauté the chopped mushrooms in the olive oil for several minutes. Add the leeks, parsley, lemon juice, cooked beans and seasoning. Place the cooked pasta in the bottom of a dish and spoon the vegetable mixture over the top. Melt the butter in a pan and stir in the flour. Gradually add the milk and bring to the boil, stirring all the time until the sauce begins to thicken. Remove from the heat and stir in the cream or yoghurt. Pour over the vegetables and bake for 15-20 minutes or until the dish is heated through.
   Serve as a supper dish with a fresh salad.

Nut Rolls

A delightful pastry roll filled with peanuts and vegetables. Children love them and they are always appreciated in packed lunches and on picnics.

pastry:
8 oz (2 cups) wholewheat flour
4 oz (½ cup) butter
8 teaspoons cold water
filling:
8 oz (1 cup) ground peanuts
1 large onion, chopped
2 leeks, chopped
2 carrots, grated
1 clove garlic, crushed
1 teaspoon miso
1 egg
1 tablespoon soya oil
seasoning

Preheat the oven to 375°F/190°C/Reg 5.
   Sauté the vegetables in a little oil until soft. Blend the miso with 1 tablespoon of cold water and stir into the vegetables. Add the ground nuts and season to taste. Lightly beat the egg and mix with the other ingredients. The mixture should be slightly sticky, extra milk or water can be added if it looks too dry.

Make the pastry and roll out into an oblong measuring approximately 9 inches by 6 inches. Divide the pastry into 2 long strips and place a sausage shaped piece of filling down the centre of each. Dampen the pastry edges with water, roll up the pastry and cut into 2 inch lengths. Brush the tops with a little beaten egg and bake for 30-40 minutes.

Corn Mexacali

Maize was held in high esteem by the American Indians; both sweetcorn and maize meal are often used in the cuisine of the Southern States. In this dish, golden coloured corn bread tops a rich, juicy bean base. The flavour of the corn is complemented and enhanced by the savoury qualities of the blackeye beans and the richness of the soya sauce.

4 oz (½ cup) blackeye beans
½ pt (1¼ cups) water

Cook the beans until tender. Drain and reserve the bean stock.

filling:
6 oz (1 cup) sweet corn
1 onion
1 clove of garlic
1 tablespoon olive oil
1 tablespoon soya sauce
½ teaspoon thyme
½ teaspoon marjoram
4 tablespoons bean stock

topping:
4 oz (1 cup) maize meal
¼ pt (½ cup) natural yoghurt
1 egg beaten
½ pt (1¼ cups) milk
1 tablespoon butter
1 teaspoon baking powder
seasoning

Preheat the oven to 450°F/230°C/Reg 8.
Chop the onion and garlic and sauté in the olive oil until transparent. Add the sweetcorn, bean stock, thyme, marjoram, soya sauce and beans. Simmer gently for 5 minutes before placing in a deep dish.
Put the maize meal and baking powder into a bowl. Melt the butter in a pan and when cool add the yoghurt, the beaten egg and milk. Pour these ingredients into the bowl containing the flour and mix together well. Spoon the topping over the bean mixture and bake for 30 minutes or until the corn bread is a deep, golden colour and pulls away from the sides of the dish.
Serve for supper or luncheon with lemon buttered mushrooms and french beans.

Falafel

A popular dish in the Middle East where it is deep fried until the outside puffs up and becomes crispy. It is eaten as a snack, sandwiched between pitta bread.

8 oz (1 cup) chick peas, soaked and drained
2 pts (5 cups) water

Cook the beans until soft. Drain and mash.

2 cooked potatoes, mashed
1 large onion
4 tablespoons chopped parsley/coriander
1 tablespoon natural yoghurt
1 tablespoon tahini
1 tablespoon olive oil
½ teaspoon cayenne
½ teaspoon paprika
1 clove of garlic
juice of 1 lemon
seasoning

Preheat the oven to 350°F/180°C/Reg 4.

Chop the onion and garlic finely and sauté in the olive oil until transparent. Combine all the ingredients and adjust the seasoning to taste. If the mixture is too soft stir in a little wholewheat flour. Form into small, flat cakes, and deep fry or place on a greased baking tray and cook for 20-25 minutes until lightly brown on both sides.

Serve with a lettuce, cucumber and tomato salad tossed in olive oil and garnished with black olives. Savoury pancake rolls and a tahini dip could complete the meal.

Boston Baked Beans

8 oz (1 cup) haricot beans, soaked and drained
1 pt (2½ cups) water

Cook the beans for half the recommended time.

1 large cooking apple, sliced
1 onion, chopped
½ inch fresh root ginger, bruised
1 teaspoon mustard
1 tablespoon molasses
1 tablespoon sunflower oil

Preheat the oven to 400°F/200°C/Reg 6.

Heat the oil in a pan and lightly fry the apple, onion and ginger. Place them in a casserole and add the remaining ingredients. Cover the dish and bake for 1 hour or until the beans are tender. Bake uncovered for a further 10 minutes before serving.

Home-Made Tomato Sauce

1 lb (2 cups) ripe tomatoes
3 large spring onions, finely chopped
1 bay leaf
1 teaspoon paprika
1 teaspoon oregano
¼ teaspoon cayenne pepper
juice of 1 lemon
seasoning

Spear the tomatoes with a fork and rotate over an open flame. Remove the tomato skins and chop well. Put them in a pan with the onions and simmer gently for 5 minutes. Add the remaining ingredients and cook for 10 minutes more before seasoning to taste.

The sauce can be rubbed through a sieve or whisked in a blender if a creamier consistency is required.

Mediterranean Bean Loaf

A colourful, moist bean loaf that can be eaten
hot or cold.

6 oz (¾ cup) red kidney beans, soaked and
drained
1½ pts (3¾ cups) water

Cook the beans until tender. Drain and mash to
form a smooth purée.

4 oz (1½ cups) mushrooms
3 oz (¾ cup) fresh wholewheat breadcrumbs
1 oz (½ cup) wheatgerm
1 green pepper
1 leek
1 clove of garlic
1½ tablespoons tomato purée
1½ tablespoons soya sauce
1 tablespoon olive oil
1 teaspoon mixed herbs

Preheat the oven to 400°F/200°C/Reg 6.
   Slice the vegetables and fry lightly in the olive
oil. Mix all the ingredients together, adding only
sufficient breadcrumbs and wheatgerm to ensure
a firm but moist consistency. Place in a greased
1 lb loaf tin and bake for 1-1¼ hours.
   Serve with sautéed courgettes, wholewheat
spaghetti and a home-made tomato sauce.

Desserts

Apricot Cheese Cake

Fresh apricots are available in many good fruit shops during the summer months. The stones are easily removed and there is little wastage. Dried apricots can be used in their place where necessary.

base:
4oz (½ cup) butter
2 oz (¾ cup) porridge oats
1 oz (¼ cup) wholewheat flour
1 oz (¼ cup) oat flakes
1 oz (½ cup) desiccated coconut
filling:
4 tablespoons tofu
4 oz (½ cup) curd cheese/cottage cheese
¼ pt (½ cup) natural yoghurt
2 eggs
2 teaspoons gelatine/arrowroot
2-3 tablespoons honey
1 tablespoon orange juice
topping:
½ lb fresh apricots
½ pt (1¼ cups) water
3 tablespoons orange juice
2 teaspoons gelatine

Preheat the oven to 400°F/200°C/Reg 6.

To make the base rub the fat into the dry ingredients and press in a greased, loose bottomed cake tin. Place in the oven and bake until golden brown on top. Put aside to cool.

To make the filling separate the egg yolks from the whites. Place the yolks and honey in a bowl set in a pan of gently boiling water and cook, stirring constantly, until the mixture begins to thicken. In another bowl mix 2 teaspoons of gelatine with 1 tablespoon of orange juice and heat over a pan of hot water until the gelatine has dissolved. Stir it into the egg mixture and leave to cool slightly. Blend/sieve the tofu, curd cheese and yoghurt together and mix into the egg mixture. Beat the egg whites until stiff and fold into the cheese filling and pour over the crumble base. Place in a refrigerator and leave to set.

For the topping, stone and slice the apricots and cook in the water until soft. Leave to cool. In a bowl mix together the gelatine and the orange juice and place over a pan of hot water until the gelatine has dissolved. Add to the cooked apricots and pour over the partially set cheese cake. Leave to set for 2 hours in a refrigerator.

Mock Mince Pie

Mock mince pie can be eaten all the year round and makes a refreshing change to traditional mince pies served at Christmas time. It is light, moist and juicy and can be topped with fresh cream, yoghurt or served with a mature white cheese.

pastry:
8 oz (2 cups) fine wholewheat flour
3 oz (⅓ cup) butter
2 tablespoons vegetable oil
8 teaspoons cold water
filling:
1 lb cooking apples
4 oz (1 cup) carrot, grated
4 oz (1 cup) mixed dried fruit
1 large orange
2 teaspoons mixed spice
1 tablespoon concentrated apple juice
1 teaspoon miso
a little water

Preheat the oven to 400°F/200°C/Reg 6.
Make the pastry and line a 7 inch flan dish with three quarters of the dough. Prick the pastry base with a fork and blind bake for 8-10 minutes.
Wash, core and slice the apples. Peel and chop the orange, remove the pips and place in a pan with the apple, grated carrot and dried fruit. Pour in ½ pint of water and simmer gently until the apple softens. Blend the miso with 1 tablespoon of cold water and add to the fruit mixture. Stir in the mixed spice and concentrated apple juice and spoon into the flan dish. Cover with a lattice top made from strips of the remaining pastry. Bake for 35-40 minutes.
Serve hot or cold.

Peach Whip

A light, refreshing summer dessert that has a creamy texture but is very low in calories.

3 peaches
4 tablespoons tofu
⅓ pt (1 cup) natural yoghurt
4 tablespoons concentrated orange juice
2 egg whites

Slice the peaches and lay them in the bottom of individual dishes. Keep back several slices to decorate the top of the whip.
Blend together the tofu, yoghurt and orange juice until smooth. Beat the egg whites to form stiff peaks and fold them into the yoghurt mixture. Spoon over the fruit and place the remaining slices of peach on the top.

Aduki Bean and Apple Crumble

4 oz (½ cup) aduki beans, soaked and drained
½ pt (1¼ cups) water

Cook the beans until soft. Drain and mash well.

topping:
2 oz (¾ cup) porridge oats
1 oz (½ cup) oat flakes
1 oz (¼ cup) wholewheat flour
1 oz (½ cup) desiccated coconut
3 tablespoons sunflower oil
filling:
1 lb cooking apples
½-1 teaspoon cinnamon
honey to taste

Preheat the oven to 400°F/200°C/Reg 6.
   Wash, core and slice the apples and cook in a little water until soft. Mix with the aduki beans and season with the cinnamon. Sweeten to taste and add a little water if the mixture is very dry. Place in a greased casserole.
   Mix all the topping ingredients together and spread evenly over a greased baking tray. Place in the oven and cook until the crumble turns a very light brown. Sprinkle over the apple mixture and bake for 20-25 minutes or until the top is golden brown and crunchy in texture.

Yorkshire Curd Tart

pastry:
7 oz (2 cups) fine wholewheat flour
1 oz (⅓ cup) soya flour
3 oz (⅓ cup) butter
2 tablespoons vegetable oil
8 teaspoons cold water
filling:
8 oz (1 cup) curd cheese
4 oz (½ cup) butter
4 oz (1 cup) currants
2 eggs, beaten
zest of 1 lemon
2 tablespoons honey
1 teaspoon ground nutmeg

Preheat the oven to 400°F/200°C/Reg 6.
   Make the pastry and line an 8 inch flan dish. Prick the pastry base and blind bake for 8-10 minutes.
   Melt the butter in a pan and add the currants and honey. Remove from the heat and leave to cool. Mix in the curd cheese, lemon zest, ground nutmeg and beaten eggs. Pour into the pastry case and bake in the oven for 30-35 minutes until firm to touch.
   Serve hot or cold.

Aduki Bean and Chestnut Cream

Chestnuts are very versatile nuts, having less fat and more carbohydrate than other varieties. They are really delicious in savoury and sweet recipes. Unfortunately they are only in season for a few months and it is sometimes difficult to cook all the different chestnut recipes in the time available! Although there are dried chestnuts in some shops they do not have the flavour or texture of the fresh ones. It is much nicer to wait for autumn and to roast the first nuts around the fire.

2 oz (¼ cup) aduki beans, soaked and drained
¼ pt (½ cup) water

Cook the beans until tender. Drain.

½ lb chestnuts
½ pt (1¼ cups) natural yoghurt
honey to taste

Prick the chestnuts with a sharp knife and bake in a moderate oven for 30-40 minutes. When soft allow to cool before removing the shells.

Blend the beans, chestnuts and yoghurt together and rub through a fine sieve. The nutty cream can be sweetened to taste before being placed in individual dishes.

Chill slightly before serving.

Mixed Fruit and Soya Pie

A tasty pie that is rich in food value and flavour. It is an excellent dessert to serve with a light vegetable luncheon.

6 oz (¾ cup) soya beans, soaked and drained
1½ pts (3¾ cups) water

Cook the beans until tender. Drain and mash well.

pastry:
8 oz (2 cups) fine wholewheat flour
4 oz (½ cup) butter
8 teaspoons cold water
pinch of salt
filling:
2 oz (½ cup) sultanas
1 large cooking apple
2 eggs
2 tablespoons honey
½ whole nutmeg
2 teaspoons mixed spice

Preheat the oven to 400°F/200°C/Reg 6.

Make the pastry and line a 7 inch flan dish. Prick the pastry with a fork and blind bake in the oven for 8-10 minutes.

Wash and core the apple and soften in a pan with a little water and the sultanas. Mix the soya bean purée with the cooked fruit and the mixed spice. Sweeten with honey to taste. Beat the two eggs and stir into the mixture. Spoon into the pastry case and sprinkle the top with freshly grated nutmeg. Bake for 35-45 minutes or until the pie is golden brown.

Serve hot or cold.

Fresh Pear Pudding

2 ripe dessert pears
3 oz (⅔ cup) wholewheat flour
1 oz (⅓ cup) soya flour
4 tablespoons desiccated coconut
2 oz (¼ cup) butter
1 tablespoon vegetable oil
4 tablespoons orange juice
zest of 1 orange
1 egg
1 teaspoon baking powder

Preheat the oven to 350°F/180°C/Reg 4.

Cream the butter and the oil together and blend with the beaten egg. Gradually fold in the sieved dry ingredients and the orange zest. Slice the pears and stir half the amount into the mixture. Add 2 tablespoons of orange juice and place the fairly stiff mixture into a greased cake tin. Lay the remaining slices of pear on top and bake for 1-1½ hours.

When cooked turn the pudding out of the tin and pour the remaining 2 tablespoons of orange juice over the base while hot.

Serve hot or cold with yoghurt, cream or custard.

Date Loaf

A sugarless fruit loaf that is simply delicious eaten sliced and buttered for tea.

8 oz (2 cups) wholewheat flour
1 oz (⅓ cup) soya flour
5 oz (⅔ cup) butter
8 oz (1⅓ cup) dried dates, chopped
4 tablespoons milk
1 teaspoon baking powder
1 egg, beaten
½ teaspoon cinnamon

Preheat the oven to 350°F/180°C/Reg 4.

Line a 2 lb bread tin with grease proof paper. Cook 2 oz (⅓ cup) of the chopped dates with 4 tablespoons of water until soft. Stir in the cinnamon and leave to cool.

Mix the dry ingredients together and rub in the fat. Add all the dates, the beaten egg and the milk. Place the mixture in the tin and bake in the centre of the oven for 50-60 minutes.

SAVOURY BISCUITS

There are many different types of biscuits and crackers available for serving with cheese and fruit after a meal. Try these two home-made varieties for a change, they are easy to make and store well in air-tight containers.

Oat Crackers

3 oz (1⅓ cups) wholewheat flour
3 oz (1⅓ cups) porridge oats
2 oz (¼ cup) butter
½ teaspoon bicarbonate of soda
½ teaspoon cream of tartar
1-2 tablespoons milk
2 teaspoons soya sauce
1 teaspoon mixed herbs

Preheat the oven to 350°F/180°C/Reg 4.
    Mix all the dry ingredients together and season with the herbs. Rub in the fat and add the soya sauce. Gradually stir in the milk until the mixture is of a consistency that can be rolled out. Roll out thinly on a floured board and cut into circles. Place on a greased baking tray and cook on the top shelf for 10 minutes until lightly brown.

Savoury Cheese Biscuits

6 oz (⅔ cups) wholewheat flour
4 oz (½ cup) cheese, grated
3 oz (⅓ cup) butter
1 egg yolk
1 teaspoon miso
seasoning
a little water

Preheat the oven to 350°F/180°C/Reg 4.
    Mix together the flour and the seasoning. Rub in the fat and add the grated cheese. Blend the egg yolk with the miso and stir into the mixture. Add sufficient water to give a smooth, fairly stiff dough and roll out on a floured board. Cut into biscuit shapes and place on a greased baking tray. Bake for 10-15 minutes until golden coloured.

Bean by Bean Recipe Index

nut rolls   73
mock mince pie   79
savory cheese biscuits   83

Soya — Tofu

tofu nut spread   29
tofu scrambled eggs   30
tofu garbanzo pâté   30
melon medley   42
tangerine tofu   42
peach whip   79
apricot cheese cake   78

Split Peas

mulligatawny soup   45
leek and green pea purée   48

Index